BRICK HOUSE

BRICK HOUSE

How to Defeat Student Apathy by Building a Brick House Culture

Danny Hill

Brick House
Danny Hill

JJ & Zak / Power of ICU
102 Hartman Drive
Suite G #224
Lebanon, Tennessee 37087

www.poweroficu.com

Copyeditors: Julie Duty, Amy O'Connell
Collaborator: Jayson Nave
Production Editor: Clayton Ledford

ISBN: 978-0-9856961-9-1

To my wife Debbie.

Our home is a Brick House because of your unconditional love and constant encouragement. You make everyone around you better just by being you. Love you, Deb!

Contents

BRICK HOUSE

Introduction

"I realize now, I can't not do my work."

"I realize now, I can't not do my work." This is, of course, improper grammar but I love the paradigm. It's a direct quote from Alex, a former apathetic student at Mitchell Middle School, South Dakota. Notice that I said, "Former apathetic student!" According to Mitchell principal, Brad Berens, this young man was in the habit of taking an academic siesta every day after arriving at school. The school staff would essentially babysit him every day and, of course, reluctantly move him on to the next grade level at the end of each school year. Alex started shutting down around fourth grade and grew more apathetic each year. Like all apathetic students, he was given (a zillion) speeches: "If you don't do your work, then you will not pass," and, "If you don't do your work, then you will never get a job," blah, blah, blah. But somehow, he would magically appear in the next grade without earning his way. If he had already figured out the superficial system filled with false threats, then how in the world did the Mitchell Middle School staff convince Alex to realize now that he "can't not do" his work?

Maybe this former apathetic student was walking to school one morning and someone hit him in the head with a corncob! (Mitchell is the home of the famous Corn Palace). The blow from the corncob was just enough to knock some sense into him. During first period his teacher noticed Alex was actively engaged so she praised him for his efforts. His robotic reply, "I realize now, I can't not do my work." Is this what happened? I don't think so!

Maybe Alex and several other disengaged students were administered a new Anti-Apathy Pill that turned apathetic students into over achievers. Oh, if only there was such a pill.

No, there was no pill, and no corncob. Alex was attending the same school but was experiencing an entirely new school culture. He was immersed in an environment where students were no longer let off the hook; a culture where every student was required to complete every assignment; a culture where purpose was well defined; a culture where learning the academic standards was on the top of everybody's mind every day.

Remember the story of the <u>Three Little Pigs</u>? Each pig made a choice about how to build his house. Two chose to quickly put together fragile houses. One out of sticks the other out of straw. When the Big Bad Wolf came, he easily blew both of these flimsy structures down. However, the third pig chose to take his time and build a strong fortress that nothing, including the Big Bad Wolf, could penetrate. He built a Brick House.

Mitchell Middle school built a Brick House School Culture and students changed. Just like each of the three little pigs had a choice and controlled the way they built their houses, every school controls the way they do things. Is your school culture fragile/flimsy like the houses made of sticks and straw, or a rock solid Brick House?

Throughout this book I will use this simple definition for *culture*:

The way we do things around here.

How often do you provide extra time/extra help for your students? Is the main purpose well defined and on the top of everybody's mind every day? Are you grading responsibility and deadlines? Do you keep a list of missing assignments and hold every student accountable for completing their assignments? Are parents notified daily of their children's missing work? Mitchell Middle School addressed all of these important issues and their students finally realized they "can't not do their work."

Chapter One

BRICK HOUSE

"Setting the right cultural tone is everything – and everyone is involved."
– John Miller

A fun part of our Power of ICU presentation happens when we pick someone to tell the story of the <u>Three Little Pigs</u>. This story usually creates a lot of laughter and entertainment because details are added or deleted depending on who is telling their version of this familiar children's tale. The director of schools in Rio Hondo, Texas strategically placed her chair in front of her administrators as she emphasized every detail including each pig's response to the wolf's threat, "Not by the hair of my chinny, chin, chin!" It was probably the most professional and accurate version we have experienced. However, our most entertaining <u>Three Little Pigs</u> storyteller was from Landrum Middle School in Houston, Texas. Andre, a former Texas A&M football player, relished the opportunity to juice up the story while blowing loudly into my microphone when he got to, "And the big bad wolf huffed and puffed and blew the house down!" We all felt like we were in the story for a moment and couldn't wait for the next house to be blown down because the Big Bad Wolf's breath got louder and stronger each time. Sometimes the storyteller will throw us a curveball. One teacher claimed the big bad wolf flew over the brick house in a hot air balloon in order to drop into the chimney. SERIOUSLY?

At least everyone agrees the first pig foolishly **chose** to build his house out of straw, the second pig foolishly **chose** to build his house out of sticks, and the third pig wisely **chose** to build his house out of brick. The big bad wolf was able to easily blow down the fragile straw and stick houses but not the sturdy Brick House. In the original 1950's version, the first and second pigs were eaten by the wolf. This version must have created a lot of emotional scars in those of us born in the fifties and sixties because the much softer, more politically correct seventies version had the first two pigs running next door instead of getting eaten. Can a pig outrun a wolf? If you look closely at pictures and video of the Vietnam War protests of the 1970's you can see flags being burned in the streets along with the original versions of the <u>Three Little Pigs</u> (kidding). I am presently working on an even more politically correct 21st century version where even the wolf doesn't die (endangered species). In fact, he and the <u>Three Little Pigs</u> become a Professional Learning Community (PLC) and live happily ever after!

Our first book, <u>Power of ICU...The Defeat of Student Apathy</u>, challenged schools to tear down their fragile school culture and build up a totally new and improved way of doing things. While hundreds of schools like Mitchell have been extremely successful, others have tried and either struggled or failed. This book, <u>Brick House</u>, will help struggling ICU schools identify snags and challenge the successful schools to build an even stronger school culture that is totally focused on STUDENTS LEARNING the ACADEMIC STANDARDS.

Throughout <u>Brick House</u> we will *comb through traditional thinking patterns/assumptions*. Linda Crutcher, Southside's wonderful guidance counselor and my good friend, always tells the students, "Lies will get you all tied up and tangled up, but truth will set you free." Just like a comb or brush is used to untangle our hair (not mine), TRUTH is the only way to comb the error out of our thinking. Too many teachers have shut their eyes in denial, thinking things will get better on their own, or despair, paralyzed by hopelessness. Others have lost their identity and passion. Denial and despair have one thing in common; both lead to inaction and teacher apathy.

Brick House is an action plan that works. Too many of the children who enter our schools

Denial and despair have one thing in common; both lead to inaction and teacher apathy.

every day have the Big Bad Wolf in their dysfunctional lives. Some children are born into a house made of straw/sticks with the Big Bad Wolf just waiting to blow the house down and devour them. Alcohol, drugs, poverty, and sexual assault steal our students' spirits and then they come to school hopeless. Daddy leaves, never to be heard from again and the Big Bad Wolf whispers in the child's ear every day, "It was your fault." Mom gets cancer, dad gets drunk and the Big Bad Wolf runs rampant. When the economy tanked two years ago, the campground next to our school was full of new tenants that had lost their homes. All of a sudden our school had dozens of new students who were living in tents or campers with little or no money - the Big Bad Wolf was breathing down their necks.

Dr. Doug Reeves, founder of The Leadership and Learning Center, says that when teachers "focus exclusively on external challenges (dysfunctional homes); educators are victims who wait for the impact of outside forces to exert their will on us." This is absolutely true. Teachers everywhere complain, "But what can we do about the parents? They just don't care." And, "What can we do about the students who just won't do anything?" I am constantly confronted with, "The problem in education starts in the home. The parents don't do their job and expect us to do it for them." Helplessness is alive and well in the thinking of many educators. Stop feeling helpless and get to work on the internal challenges that you do have total control over. Comb through your thinking and build a Brick House. Your apathetic and irresponsible students will soon realize "I can't not do my work!"

Chapter Two

TRUTH OR CHASING SHADOWS?
OUT OF THE CAVE AND INTO THE LIGHT

A paradigm is a model or a pattern of thinking. It is a shared set of assumptions with how we perceive the world. In *Plato's Republic*, Plato uses the *Allegory of the Cave* to illustrate the power of paradigm. Because decisions we make as teachers are based on accepted thinking patterns, what if we have error in our thinking? The *Allegory of the Cave* is written as a fictional dialogue between Plato's teacher Socrates and Plato's brother Glaucon. In the dialogue, Socrates describes a group of people (let's say educators) who have lived chained to the wall of a cave all of their lives (let's say because of the way we were taught), facing a blank wall. The people watch shadows projected on the wall by things passing in front of a fire behind them and begin to ascribe forms to these shadows. According to Socrates, they believe the shadows are authentic because they have never observed or experienced the truth.

As teachers, we have been chained to the wall of a cave in our thinking because of the way we were taught when we were students. False assumptions passed down to us within our profession make deep impressions on our paradigm. Opinions are often based on what feels right or sounds right which then control our actions. Teachers frequently say, "In real life you will be fired if you turn something in late." And, "I am just trying to teach my students about real life." If these statements are echoed by the majority of educators then they must be true. In real life, however, how many teachers in your building have been fired for turning in their daily attendance late? The county commission and school board in a nearby district were a month late in passing the county budget recently. The students had to start school two weeks late, but I wonder how many school board members or county commissioners were fired? It's hard to let go of old assumptions because they sound so convincing "on the surface."

The *Allegory of the Cave* teaches that what one takes to be real may in fact be an illusion. The prisoners watch the shadows cast by the men, not knowing they are shadows. Socrates then supposes that a prisoner is freed and permitted to stand up. If someone were to show him the three-dimensional figures that had cast the shadows, he would not recognize them for what they were and could not name them. Because of the power of paradigm he would continue to believe the shadows on the wall to be more real than what he sees right in front of him.

What if someone forcibly dragged such a man upward, out of the cave? Wouldn't the man be angry at the one doing this to him? Plato taught that any challenge to our thinking/paradigm/deep seated beliefs brings about 1) anger, and 2) fear. "Don't mess with my thinking," and, "You are entitled to your opinion," are common responses when a person's thinking is questioned. It is more comfortable to go right back to facing the wall and believing in the shadows.

Punishing students with grades as a consequence for missing assignments does not work, but as educators we can't seem to let go of this bad practice. ICU schools hold boldly to, "You still have to do it," and students soon realize, "They can't not do their work."

Evidence and truth do not always correlate with a shift in paradigm. As Plato explains, our paradigm is something we get very comfortable with. When things get messy during your culture shift the teachers whose paradigm never shifted will run right back to facing the wall and believing in the shadows. "See, I knew this would not work," is common. They may try to take others back to chasing shadows because there is comfort in numbers. Anger and fear during the mess is acceptable as long as you get out of the cave and into the light.

After some time on the surface, however, the freed prisoner would acclimate. He would see more and more things around him, until he could see that the shadows were an illusion and not the truth. Once the freed prisoner realized

He would see more and more things around him, until he could see that the shadows were an illusion and not the truth.

the error in his thinking, he could never go back to believing the shadows were real.

"I was a huge skeptic of ICU at first. It seemed to me a way to enable students to ignore deadlines and to foster laziness. I was so very wrong! It never occurred to me that for many students, a zero on an assignment was exactly what they wanted. I've been teaching for seventeen years, and this is the first year that every student in my classroom did every assignment. That has to be good for learning!

Mrs. Lorang, 7th Grade English – Pipestone Middle School

"The world is flat because it seems flat," is a simple example of error controlling one's paradigm. However, when data falls outside our paradigm, we find it hard to see and accept. Mrs. Lorang started with the assumption that ICU would, "Enable students to ignore deadlines and to foster laziness." This is an excellent example of chasing a shadow and remaining in the cave in our thinking. However, after holding students accountable at Pipestone using the ICU list, her thinking pattern changed. Based on the experience what she found was just the opposite.

There are many teachers who believe down deep in their souls that telling a student, "You cannot do the assignment now because you did not do it right the first time," teaches responsibility. They have been facing the cave wall and believing in this shadow for so long, they get angry when you point out the error in that logic. Even after I share this analogy, some continue to emotionally cling to their opinion because it just "sounds right" to them.

We all want our own children to learn to be responsible. We would never use this scenario to teach our own children responsibility. "Zach, clean your room." Five minutes later, he is back watching TV so I confront him. "Zach, you did not clean your room." He looks at me with that distant apathetic stare. "Zach, you did not clean your room, so now I am not going to let you clean it. I am trying to teach you responsibility, son, and if you don't clean your room the first time, then I am not going to let you clean it." I am sure Zach would start to cry, "Daddy, Daddy, please let me clean my room." --- Yeah right!

There is no way anybody in their right mind would ever try to teach responsibility and hold their own children accountable by letting them off the hook. In fact, this is the best way to help your child turn into a lazy bum.

I believe the biggest obstacle schools face in building a Brick House is error in thinking patterns. Can you defeat student apathy or are the students beyond help because of their dysfunctional families? If you believe the students are beyond help, then let's comb through your thinking and replace this lie with truth because student apathy can be defeated. A shift in paradigm will pave the way for a shift in culture.

Chapter Three

Declare War On Apathy

"Is it ignorance or is it apathy? I don't know and I don't care."

– Jimmy Buffett

Some schools are incapable of declaring war on student apathy because they have their own cultural civil war going on among the adults. Cliques square off, grade levels blame each other for unprepared students, some teachers resent the coaches, special education and regular education teachers argue constantly, the teachers disrespect the administration, or the administration disrespects the teachers. I am confident that student apathy can be defeated in our schools but you cannot fight two wars at once.

Before I present to a school staff, I always ask them to come up with an estimated percentage of apathetic students at their school and the number I hear most frequently is thirty-five percent. Eighty-five percent is the highest number I have heard and eighteen percent is the lowest estimate of apathetic students. For the purpose of this book, I will use thirty-five percent in referencing apathy. Without an effective plan of attack, these percentages will be the same five years from now. If you are serious about taking on student apathy, read on. This is not a rah-rah book about how to give better speeches or threats because they have little or no effect on lethargic students. This is not a book suggesting how to tweak traditional practices based on traditional thinking. Building a Brick House requires changes in the way you do things and challenges your entire staff to work together. Using the ICU list, a specific list of missing assignments, you eliminate threats and speeches completely which reduces teacher stress.

Leave Me Alone

Apathy is defined as a lack of passion or emotion. A person labeled as apathetic appears to lack interest or concern for things others find moving or exciting and their body language cries, "Leave Me Alone." He does not care if you threaten a zero, he does *Arm yourselves with the ICU list and Never Leave Them Alone* not care if you threaten failure, he is deaf to your speeches, and constantly thinking just "Leave Me Alone."

Apathetic parents tell you to stop bothering them at work or at home. "I sleep all day and cannot be disturbed, so in the future please just 'Leave Me Alone.'"

Apathetic teachers who checked out emotionally years ago want to go to their classroom and shut their door so they can do their own thing. They might as well hang a sign on their door that says, "Please Leave Me Alone." (At least they say please.)

Never Leave Them Alone

Always follow this Golden Rule to defeat apathy:

What do we do about apathetic students?
Never Leave Them Alone

What do we do about apathetic parents?
Never Leave Them Alone

What do we do about apathetic teachers?
Never Leave Them Alone

Arm yourselves with the ICU list and Never Leave Them Alone

A weapon, arm, or armament is a tool or instrument used in order to inflict damage to the enemy. Your enemy is apathy (*not* the student). Effective tools/instruments include anything that will gain a strategic or mental advantage over an adversary.

A brick house school culture includes all of the effective tools necessary to defeat apathy. However, the ICU List is the most powerful instrument that will give you a strategic and mental advantage. Stop believing there is nothing you can do if a student doesn't care. The list of missing assignments replaces the speeches and threats. There is power in a list!

A student at Pipestone Middle School told me, "Mr. Hill, last year I was on the ICU list every day, but this year I am never on the list." The young man was grinning and very proud of himself. I asked, "Why are you not on the list this year? What changed?" He very quickly responded, "I just decided it's much easier to stay off the list than to be on the list." Student apathy can and must be defeated.

Mike Ford, Assistant Principal at Jackson Junior High (eighth and ninth grades) in Jackson, Missouri overheard a Jackson ninth grader telling a new student, "You might as well do your work the first time because at this school they will bug you to death if you don't." Jackson Junior High teachers made a commitment to build (not try to build) a Brick House, which never leaves any student alone. Student paradigm changed as a result of the unified staff effectively using their ICU list to win the war on apathy. Since the war ended at Jackson Junior High, Principal Cory Crosnoe and his team know how to work together, solve problems, and analyze data. Knowing that *every student will complete every assignment* has empowered them to have higher expectations for their students to learn the academic standards instead of just doing the work.

The war is not teacher vs. student. Staff members cannot allow themselves to get angry and take it personally when students do not complete assignments. This is a waste of precious time and energy. United, all staff members must aggressively attack and defeat the cancerous indifference that kills the spirit of our students. Apathy has infected our schools and drained the passion out of excellent teachers. Before finding a cure for any disease, scientists and doctors examine the root cause. Within a few months of starting ICU, one teacher commented, "We have always had the problem (student apathy) …but now we have a specific and targeted plan in place to deal with it!"

In a Brick House, the remedy for student apathy is to <u>Never Leave Them Alone</u>.

Chapter Four

THERE IS POWER IN THE LIST

"The only way to hold every student accountable for completing every assignment is with a list."

– Danny Hill

List Lists

At the beginning of every presentation I give teachers three minutes to work individually or in groups to list as many lists as they can. They easily come up with a dozen or more lists adults use in real life on a regular basis to hold themselves accountable. Shopping list, Christmas list, list of birthdays, list of bills to pay, and a bucket list are always given. One guy in Texas shouted out, "I keep a list of sins," which sort of threw me for a loop. Recently in Carlsbad, New Mexico, a young woman said, "Honey-Do List," to which a number of women nodded in agreement. I said, "Did you happen to leave your honey a list of things to do today?" She enthusiastically responded, "I leave him a list every single day. If I don't then he won't do anything. He'll use the old 'I forgot' excuse when I get home." Another lady spoke up, "And if you want him (your honey) to complete his assignments for the day, you better put the list in the two places he will be sure and see it – on the refrigerator and the wide screen TV."

In the adult world, successful wives understand that verbally telling their husbands their work assignments brings poor results. Placing the "Honey- Do" list on the television and on the refrigerator where they are clearly visible for the husband eliminates, "I forgot," as an option. Wise husbands check off each assignment after completion. I briefly ask, "If you leave your grocery shopping list at home…?" The audience will shout, "Then you will surely forget something!" And as you pick up an item from the shelf and put it in your shopping cart…?" They respond, "You check it off." My summary statement to the group is usually something like, "Are we in agreement then? Adults need lists to hold us <u>accountable</u> and to be <u>responsible</u> for completing tasks?" To which there is unanimous agreement.

At Southside, we discovered the power of lists by accident. As explained in <u>Power of ICU</u>, Toni Eubanks, a consultant with the Southern Region Education Board, challenged us to "stop letting students off the hook" when they do not complete assignments. We thought the only possible consequence for missing assignments was "punishment by grades." However, after much discussion over the summer, we decide to:

1. Stick to our guns
2. Hold students accountable
3. Stop letting students off the hook
4. Give back incomplete or unacceptable work
5. Incomplete missing assignments would not affect grades

Every assignment would be completed. It sounded easy enough! (Were we naïve or what?)

During the first week of school, things started to get a little messy. When students (lots of them) would fail to turn in assignments, our staff would simply respond, "You still have to do it." We were doing what we had committed to do: no let them off the hook- right? After two weeks of "sticking to our guns," the mess was already getting out of hand. Although teachers appeared confident while the students were there, we all fell apart after they left. Fear and anger were replacing our excitement and high expectations. What were we thinking? What have we gotten ourselves into? We were treading water and starting to sink!

By the end of week three our situation was totally out of control. Apathetic students were still not doing their work and all the other students kept wondering, "HOW are the teachers going to make the 'lazy students' do their work?" We weren't even close to being able to give poor quality work back, because we were drowning in make-up work. Our staff met every day after school and would brainstorm about how to make this work. We had two choices, give up and throw in the towel or dig in and find some answers. I will never forget one of my teachers summarizing our mess. "We don't even know who owes us what." Another chimed in with, "And the students don't even know what they owe."

After a few more moments of venting frustration (many on the verge of tears), one of the teachers said, "I wonder if it would help if we started keeping a list? If we write the missing assignments down on a list, at least everybody would know who owes what. Do you think that might help?" Nobody clapped, smiled, or got excited but we made one critical decision that day, we were not throwing in the towel. We were going to find some answers and keeping a list was our only

The ICU list was the catalyst that stimulated change and the glue that held us together.

possible solution. How could something as simple as keeping a list of missing assignments empower us to "stop letting students off the hook?" What did we have to lose?

Mike Presley, our 8th grade math teacher, offered to set up an Excel spreadsheet to use as our list and we agreed to call it the ICU list (your grade is sick and needs intensive care). Mike's original ICU list was brilliant! Although our condition remained chaotic for months, the more we depended on the list, the more our mess started to clear up. Teachers would make suggestions, like color coding certain groups of students, and Mike would tweak the list. We learned that the list must be accurate, updated daily, and accessible to everyone. The ICU list was the catalyst that stimulated change and the glue that held us together. Although it was hard work, every student completed every assignment. The quality of work continued to improve and the majority of assignments were turned in on time.

Although we never made "NO ZEROS" a policy, we eliminated the need for them. We won the war on apathy at Southside and the next step for school improvement came naturally. Now that every student was completing every assignment, we could totally focus on every student learning the academic standards. The shift from students' "doing their work" to "learning the academic standards" felt really good to teachers, students, and parents.

School improvement can seem more like spinning your wheels in the mud than effectively advancing your school culture. You plan all summer and have great ideas about school improvement and then nothing takes root. It seems like once the year starts and the students arrive you begin treading water and regress back into survival mode. Why do the students have to show up and ruin everything? (Just kidding.) Often, a month into the school year your "improvement plan" disappears like a vapor. This will not happen because the ICU list works as a catalyst and glue. In other words, if you decide to use *Every Student Completes Every Assignment* as your foundation, then the list is your superglue and fuel.

"I totally agree that the ICU list is the necessary catalyst for building a new culture. It is not the answer by itself. We do so many things to help support our students, but without the ICU List there is no doubt in my mind that our dropout rate would be higher. ICU is the cement that holds everything together. Every staff member works the list every day and every student completes every assignment."

Principal Phil Rogers, South Gibson County High School

Chapter Five

EVERY STUDENT COMPLETES EVERY ASSIGNMENT

THE FOUNDATION FOR YOUR BRICK HOUSE

Do you believe every student should complete every assignment? Of course! Then use *every student completes every assignment* as your foundation and start holding students accountable. Teachers are constantly being told we need to have "higher expectations" for our students, but in class we have several students who are asleep before the tardy bell rings every day. Apathy is the anchor that keeps dragging our classroom culture down. *Every student completes every assignment* is an attainable and measurable goal that lifts the anchor so you can move forward.

We had lots of transient students at Southside so we placed a lot of emphasis on how to handle the registration process. Here is how we laid the foundation with new students:

1. Our secretary would greet the new parent and student, hand them a registration form, and at some point let them know that, "At Southside *every student completes every assignment.*"

2. After the registration form was completed our registrar, would take the student into the conference room to assess the student's math and reading levels. At some point she would say, "By the way, at Southside *every student completes every assignment.*"

3. One of our counselors would set up a class schedule and get to know the student. While escorting the new student to their first class she would say, "I'm sure you have already heard this, but be sure you complete all of your assignments because at Southside *every student completes every assignment.*"

4. Often, during lunch, some of the students would tell the new student, "Be sure you do your work, because they make you do your work here."

5. Every teacher would repeat, *"Every student completes every assignment,"* as the foundation statement throughout the day.

Our foundation statement was non-threatening and our tone was always firm but friendly. Generally, our transient students were completing their assignments within two weeks.

In building a strong culture, this (100% completion) is a perfect foundation to build upon because it is something parents and teachers agree on. *Every student completes every assignment* is common, solid ground for all stakeholders. Parents will argue over grades and behavior issues, 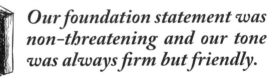 *Our foundation statement was non-threatening and our tone was always firm but friendly.* but even the most extreme parents will agree that they expect their child to "do the work." Minnesota's Glencoe Silver Lake principal, Paul Sparby, and assistant principal, Daniel Svoboda, emailed me recently after two months of persistence with the parents and students using the list for assignment completion:

"It was just like you said, Danny, parents will not argue about completing assignments like they used to about grades and behavior. All parents are on board, and I mean all! The students realize the parents are backing the teachers now and they are just giving in one by one. We are already seeing a significant change in many of our students."

Students must learn the academic standards. **Assuming your assignments are significant and directly tied to the standards,** how can you allow them a choice? If assignments are the necessary "practice" for learning the academic standards, then you cannot allow anyone to choose to miss "practice." "Practice makes perfect" is a pretty solid old saying for coaches, band directors, choir directors, and play directors. Is this a wise approach for all teachers to use? Absolutely! "You can't miss math practice," sounds pretty good. "You need extra practice on multiplying fractions," is perfect language.

Remember, students have been given a choice for years in completing assignments. They have learned to wait out your threats until you let them have their way – off the hook. Student paradigm must shift and this takes patience and consistency by all staff members. They believe down deep in their thinking that failure is an option. At Southeast Middle School in Diamond, Ohio, students put up a sign in the hallway within a month after starting ICU:

At a school in Tennessee, a group of high school students created a petition against ICU. The petition read, "*ICU steps on our Constitutional Right to come to school and do nothing.*" Stop laughing.

Where did our students get the idea (paradigm) that "failure is their choice," or that coming to school and doing nothing is their "Constitutional Right?" We say things like, "Well, you are old enough now to decide for yourself. If you chose to just sit there, then…" I have heard this approach repeatedly used with high school and middle school students. "You are a teenager. You are old enough to make up your own mind. If you chose to fail, then that is on you." Maybe we should take this approach on down to kindergarten and preschool. "If you old enough to walk, then you are old enough to make up your own mind about learning your A, B, Cs." AHHHH!

In The Case against Zeros, Dr. Doug Reeves says that one of the most important issues that teachers wrestle with (and argue about) is, "To determine the appropriate consequence for students who fail to complete an assignment." (Phi Delta Kappa, Vol. 86, No 4, Dec 2004, pp. 324-325). He says, "The most common answer is to punish these students. There is almost a fanatical belief that punishment through grades will motivate students, even though there is evidence to the contrary." In contrast, Reeves says, "There are at least a few educators experimenting with the notion that the appropriate consequence for failing to complete an assignment is to require the student to complete the assignment."

In a Brick House school, teachers are all on the same page. *Punishing by grades* and *every student completes every assignment* mix like oil and water. There is no neutral ground and one teacher cannot decide to do his own thing. You cannot win the war on student apathy if there is a civil war going on with some teachers clinging to the *punishment through grades* consequence while others say all assignments are important and must be completed. As a staff, make a choice and agree to abide by the decision. Unity of the staff is critical to student success. *Every student completes every assignment* is a rock solid foundation to build upon.

"No studies support the use of low grades or marks as punishment. Instead of promoting greater effort it more often causes students to withdraw from learning."

Guskey, T. & Bailey, J. (2001). *Developing Grading and Reporting Systems for Student Learning. Thousand Oaks, CA: Corwin Press.*

Don't *try* this

You don't *try* to build a new house, you either build it or you don't. ICU is not just another phase or initiative you *try* for a while. Would you invest a lot of time and money into opening a new restaurant and *try* to make it successful? Your chances of having a successful marriage

You don't try to build a new house, you either build it or you don't.

are slim if you tell your fiancé, "I'll *try* to make this marriage work." In education we tend to *try* the latest idea that will fix our school. Do not *try* to build a Brick House school culture or you will have little chance of defeating student apathy. Commitment to build is critical. Your approach as a staff is critical. If you are going to war, you must be united. "A house divided against itself cannot stand." You are building a culture, not trying some new idea.

"Individual commitment to a group effort – that is what makes a team work." - Vince Lombardi

What if you and the majority of your staff were physically building a house together? Everyone was working hard, some painting, others laying brick, but five or six staff members were standing there watching, not helping. Not only were they not helping, they were pointing out your mistakes. "That paint color is ugly. That board is crooked. We can't believe you chose brick instead of sticks and straw – bricks take so much longer." You would tell them to zip it and to either help build or move to another house.

One principal recently contacted me saying, "Our students keep waiting for one of their teachers to 'blink' but it is not going to happen. We are totally committed." The war on apathy will be over soon and the teachers will be able to totally focus their energy on each student learning the academic standards.

A superintendent of schools said a middle school teacher overheard one of her students at McDonald's a couple of weeks into the new school year. The 8th grader said, "Mom, I guess I am going to have to start doing all my work this year. They have this new thing called ICU where they keep a list and you have to keep your list cleaned off."

At another school, the staff took a vote after I completed my <u>Power of ICU</u> presentation. The teacher who called for the vote encouraged them to either build it together or just leave it alone. He said, "Let's not just TRY IT." Due to the strong commitment of the staff, students changed dramatically. In fact, within a few weeks a group of student leaders asked for a meeting. Their opening statement was, "OK, we get it. We understand that we have to start doing our work, but could we please discuss the lunch ICU time? We don't like to miss out on eating lunch with our friends." The principal called me and said, "Danny, the War on Apathy is over!"

Chapter Six

THESE KIDS ARE SO IRRESPONSIBLE!

Irresponsible Teachers

While I was speaking to about eighty high school teachers recently, the Superintendent of Schools addressed the teachers. He was direct but respectful as he spoke. "I agree with everything Danny has presented so far this morning. I bought the book, <u>Power of ICU</u>, for each one of you about a month ago. I told you that I would pay you each a stipend if you read the book and then turned in a short summary of your thoughts, questions, and feedback on it. Last Monday was the due date for your summaries to be turned in to me. Please raise your hand if you did not have your summary turned in by the due date." Of the eighty teachers, about twenty of them raised their hands. I was floored! He said, "Since many of you take off points for late work, I guess I should reduce the $100 stipend by $10 per day. I have heard many of you argue that you do not take late work because you would get fired if you did not meet a deadline with your boss, so I guess some of you should receive a pink slip." The room was dead silent and several teachers looked uncomfortable. He continued, "I am not going to do that. In fact, on Wednesday of this week I visited all twenty of you and personally asked for your summaries so I could pay you because I want all of you to learn from the book and get your money." He told me later that two teachers had still not turned in their summaries and sounded just like students saying, "I keep forgetting, but will have it tomorrow."

I am sure that some of the teachers who turned their book summary in on time were thinking the others' pay should be reduced. I was even leaning that way a little bit because it just "seemed right/felt right." Maybe the two who turned theirs in last and had to be hounded should have their stipend cut in half or maybe receive no money at all? Remember that truth will set you free from the error in your thinking and that is what happened next. The superintendent's final statement was simple yet powerful. He stated, "My main purpose in having all of you read the book was for all of us to LEARN about <u>Power of ICU</u> and to stir your thinking before we heard Danny's presentation. All of you will receive full pay for completing the task and learning the material in his book."

Irresponsible Government

At the writing of this book our national debt in the United States is over 14 trillion dollars. Although we have a variety of political views, we all agree that our government has been IRRESPONSIBLE with our spending in America for too long. Remember the politicians that are irresponsible with our money are the very same people who keep passing new legislation to FIX EDUCATION! (Just had to vent.)

Irresponsible Households

Here are several alarming American consumer debt statistics: (Business Insider, Inc.)

- The average consumer carries four credit cards, while the average household carries $6,500 of credit card debt.

- Over 2 million American households carry more than $20,000 in credit card debt.

- 2–2.5 million Americans seek the help of a credit counselor each year to avoid bankruptcy.

Irresponsible Society

For years an irresponsible society would not buckle their seat belts even though there was strong evidence buckling up would help save lives. Many of us were raised without wearing seat belts and we just could not get into the habit even when it became the law. What finally got everyone's attention is that very irritating BEEP, BEEP, BEEP that continues until the seat belt is fastened. The loud noise will tenaciously stay after and *Never Leave You Alone* until you develop responsibility and start buckling up.

Teachers, government, households, and society in general represent the real world. If teachers think that teaching students responsibility is their primary job, then they are taking on one of societies biggest problems and this is an unattainable goal. In other words, we are chasing a shadow, and we all know you can never catch a shadow. No wonder we are exhausted and frustrated.

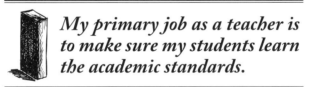

My primary job as a teacher is to make sure my students learn the academic standards.

Drive this deeply into your thinking:

My primary job as a teacher is NOT TO FIX IRRESPONSIBILITY.

My primary job as a teacher is to make sure my students learn the academic standards.

Since this is attainable and measurable, it can be a motivator for you and your students.

Chapter Seven

GRADING RESPONSIBILITY: THE DARKEST SHADOW

"Why did you take off 10 points for not putting his name on his paper?"

"I'm just trying to teach him to be responsible!"

"Why won't you accept the assignment/project late?

"I'm just trying to teach her responsibility!"

"My child earned a 95% after he restudied and retested on the Solar System, why did he receive a 75% credit?"

"I'm trying to teach him responsibility. Maybe next time he will try harder the first time!"

Isn't this a classic statement that feels right and seems right? I said the same thing hundreds of times as an 8th and 9th grade science teacher in the 1980s. In speaking to thousands of educators across the country and receiving feedback from hundreds of schools, I believe this is the darkest shadow we continue to chase and it is wearing us out.

Quick Sand

Imagine that my son has you for seventh grade science. You are an excellent teacher and my son really likes you. He turns in his science project one day after the due date but it is perfect. He gets 100% with ten points off for being late.

Written at the top: **100-10(late) = 90%**.

Our conversation goes something like this…

Danny (parent): "I know Zach's project was late but why did you count off ten percent?"

Teacher: "I am trying to teach Zach responsibility"

Danny: "I thought a grade was supposed to reflect what he has learned. So does the ninety percent represent what he has learned or is it a mixture of things - I am confused?"

Teacher: "Well, it just doesn't seem fair to the other students who turned theirs in on time for Zach to receive the same grade."

Danny: "I am not concerned about the other students and the fair is a place we go to every summer with rides and cotton candy. I just want my son to receive a grade that reflects what he knows. I still cannot figure out what the ninety percent means."

The teacher is in quick sand and sinking fast. The parent is on solid ground.

Shift your paradigm!

Character Counts

Grading responsibility wears teachers out, skews grades, and has done absolutely nothing to solve the student apathy monster. If grading responsibility is okay, then why don't we start grading loyalty? Developing loyalty in our students is very important. If a student is disloyal to one of his friends, his grade might be lowered to "teach him a lesson." Kindness is very important. If a student is unkind to another student her grade must be lowered or she might remain unkind for the rest of her life. Extremely kind students should receive higher grades of course. Is responsibility more important than trustworthiness? Is responsibility more important than kindness and loyalty? We all agree that character counts. The question is, why should we assume that it is an acceptable practice to grade responsibility and not the other important character traits that count? No matter how uncomfortable it is at first, stop grading responsibility.

- Is responsibility a state standard?

- When your students take their achievement tests, how many questions are there about "responsibility?"

- How were your "value added" (improvement scores) in responsibility?

"Teachers turn things in late all the time, as do workers in every profession. The idea that, 'You can't get away with turning work in late in the real world, Mister' isn't true."

Wormeli, R. (2006). Fair Isn't Always Equal: Assessing & Grading in the Differentiated Classroom. Portland, ME: Stenhouse Publishers.

Chapter Eight

REAL LIFE

Responsibility and accountability are learned traits that too many of our students are missing. In a Brick House culture, we teach students these important qualities without using grades as our weapon of choice. Matt Lacy, principal at Jackson Middle School, recently sent me this email after several months of keeping an ICU list and building a new culture.

"I agree that we don't grade responsibility. In fact, the cool part of ICU is that we are finally teaching kids responsibility by holding them accountable and making them do their work/learn the standards. I've had this conversation several times with staff members this year."

The reason "we are finally teaching kids responsibility" is because ICU uses proven strategies from professional bill collectors, experts in dealing with apathy, and financial advisors, experts in teaching responsibility.

Teach your students to approach their assignments as their personal debt and that those debts must be paid (Accountability/Responsibility/Engagement).

YOUR MISSING ASSIGNMENTS = YOUR PERSONAL DEBT

Two real life examples:

1. <u>Bill Collectors</u> are experts in dealing with apathy.

   The primary purpose of professional bill collectors is to get apathetic adults who owe money to pay up. If we teach students that their missing assignments are like owing debts, then we need to also teach them what happens in real life when a debt is not paid.

> A. NEVER LEAVE YOU ALONE - Bill collection agencies call you three times a day, every day. They are tenacious and one of their key strategies to get apathetic adults who owe money to pay is to bug them to death until they decide to pay.

 The golden rule to follow in dealing with student apathy is simply to Never Leave Them Alone.

Because student apathy = Leave Me Alone, the golden rule to follow in dealing with student apathy is simply to Never Leave Them Alone. Southeast Middle School (6th-8th grades) in Diamond, Ohio implemented the ICU list in March of 2012 for the final nine-week grading period. I was asked to present February 25th to the entire staff because they were fed up with student apathy and ready to do something about it. I was so impressed with their success by mid-May that I challenged the staff to see if they could be the first school to get 100% completion in their first attempt. I told them if they did it, they would have "SWAGGER" and something to brag about all summer. Here is the email I received from Mat Prezioso, the ICU lead teacher at Southeast, on June 6, 2012. It was titled: SOUTHEAST SWAGGER!

Danny,
Our seventh and eighth grade students and their teachers had their lists totally cleaned up two days before school was out. By the last day of school we only had 9 missing assignments school-

wide and we were determined to get all of them. However, two of the students on the ICU list were absent from school. Instead of giving up, we called home and one student came in immediately and completed every assignment. We called the other student but only got the machine so we kept calling. She eventually showed up at one o'clock but could not stay. We gave her the missing assignments and told her they must be turned in or she would not have a report card or a grade level to report to the next year. Surprisingly, she showed up the next morning with all of her assignments. They were checked by her teachers and deemed acceptable. WE DID IT! All assignments completed by every student for the 4th nine weeks, our first official ICU grading period!!!!!!!!

Do you see the resemblance between debt collectors "bugging you to death" and the techniques used by the excellent staff at Southeast Middle School? Notice in the email Mat says, "We were determined to get all of them," and, "Instead of giving up, we called…we kept calling." There is power in a list if you use it to NEVER LEAVE STUDENTS ALONE.

B. NEVER LET YOU OFF THE HOOK

How long would a collection agency stay in business if they used this approach?

Imagine that I had received notification from a collection agency that I owed $525 but they would not let me pay. Their first letter to me stated, "We will NOT allow you to pay the $525 now because you did not meet our deadline in paying it. We are trying to teach you about real life. We are trying to teach you how to be responsible and how to meet deadlines." Of course I would be thrilled that they would not let me pay. Never let your students off the hook and their paradigm will shift.

"When we first started ICU, I had students beg me to give them a zero. I have seen a change in my students. Those students who used to not do their work in the hope that they could just 'take the zero' now do not have that option and therefore are completing every assignment. More importantly, they are now demonstrating that they do know the material."

Mrs. Fencile, 8th and 9th Grade Math (Pipestone, MN)

2. **Personal Finance Advisors are experts in teaching responsibility**

    <u>The Total Money Makeover: A Proven Plan for Financial Success</u> is just one of the many excellent books written by Dave Ramsey. He is a financial author, radio/television host, and arguably the most popular financial expert of our time. His methods have helped millions of Americans get out of debt and develop long-term financial responsibility.

    In a recent interview, he said, "To get started you must write out all of your debts on a list." Next, he instructs his readers to, "Pay off your smallest debt first and continue paying off one debt at a time, least to greatest." He says that when people pay off one debt and then another and another it gives them the momentum to continue until all debt is paid off. He calls this the "Debt Snowball Effect."

It makes perfect sense to use the ICU list of missing assignments with your students the same way Dave Ramsey uses the list of debt. Dave teaches financial responsibility and we teach (not grade) academic responsibility. Your students will learn that in real life being late with a payment does not let you off the hook.

Academic CPR

Apathetic students have little or no academic pulse. Academic CPR revives student engagement by applying the effective techniques of bill collectors and financial advisors. To resuscitate an apathetic student follow these five steps:

STEP 1   Ask the student, "Can you tell me what you owe?"

STEP 2   Ask the student, "Is your list accurate?"

STEP 3   Ask the student, "What is the easiest assignment on your list?" (Snowball Effect)

STEP 4   Have the student actively take part in removing her first few assignments after completion.

STEP 5   Celebrate the student being totally caught up.

STEP 1

Ask the student "Can you tell me what you owe?"

This is an excellent "first step" to get the student engaged. While doing a recent follow up visit, the teachers asked me to speak with a 7th grade girl named Stephanie. I asked her if she could tell me what she owed without looking at her list. She immediately 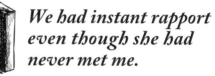 *We had instant rapport even though she had never met me.* said, "PE checklist, science project on flowers, um…oh yeah, a math assignment for Mr. Hoover, and uh…social studies redo." She was so proud and I praised her immediately for knowing her list. We had instant rapport even though she had never met me. "OK, Stephanie," I said, "let's take a look at the list together." Just like the first step toward getting out of debt is to list your debt, Stephanie must first see that the assignments are missing but not forgotten. Apathetic students have no academic heartbeat. Once a student is able to tell you what she owes, there is a faint heart beat and hope for recovery.

STEP 2

Ask the student, "Is your list accurate?"

I ask her, "Stephanie, are there any assignments on the list that have been turned in already? Is the list accurate?" This proactive approach says to the student, "We want to get it right." (Many times students will say their list is accurate; however, sometimes they will say they turned an assignment in and the teacher forgot to remove it.) The most important aspect is the "conversation" itself because it engages the student. In a Brick House, managing and addressing questions about the accuracy of the list builds a constant line of trust and communication. Remember that your target is apathy/irresponsibility. If you can get the student discussing the accuracy of "their missing assignment list," it is a positive step and the academic heartbeat begins to get stronger.

STEP 3

Ask the student, "What is the easiest assignment on your list?"
(Snowball Effect)

After listing your debt, Dave Ramsey tells you to list your debt from smallest to largest before starting to pay any of it. The "snowball effect" is exactly what we have observed time and time again with our students cleaning up their assignments one at a time and watching the lists get smaller and smaller. To get 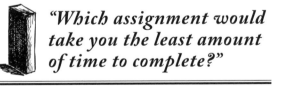 *"Which assignment would take you the least amount of time to complete?"* the ball rolling, ask the student, "What is the easiest assignment on your list?" Or, "Which assignment would take you the least amount of time to complete?" Completing one assignment at a time from "their list" is just like adults paying off their smallest debt first.

Adults who have used this method say that the "debt snowball" was a big motivator. They say that trying to eliminate or repair the whole problem by paying off the sum total of their debt was too overwhelming and it caused them to shut down. Once the student answers the question, "What is the easiest assignment on your list," you've got the pulse resuscitated and the intrinsic heartbeat of success revived so keep the rhythm going! Immediately after he has completed one assignment, have them pick another and another until they are all completed.

Research indicates that when we move closer to achieving a goal it triggers a part of the brain linked to motivation. (Csikszentmihalyi, 1997)

STEP 4

Have the student actively take part in removing her first few assignments after completion.

The student must be actively engaged in the elimination of each assignment until his academic heartbeat strengthens. Physically eliminating the first few assignments can be accomplished in a variety of ways. *Be Creative.* If you are using an iPad or computer, let her push the delete button. Several of my teachers, in addition to the school-wide database, would write names and assignments owed specifically in their classes on their whiteboard as a visible reminder. The teacher would simply have the student go to the board and erase the assignment once it was checked and deemed acceptable. My favorite for the most apathetic students is to have them write the assignment down on a piece of paper, have them rip it up, and slam dunk the completed assignment in the trash can (not every assignment of course).

STEP 5

Celebrate the student being totally caught up.

Talk to adults who have labored to pay off thousands of dollars, one debt at a time, and they will tell you they have no desire to go back in to debt. More importantly, they have developed new habits to prevent them from getting back in the financial hole.

Students that started with no
academic pulse will rush to tell every
adult that stayed after them, "I'm
all caught up!" Do you know how
much work and discipline it takes 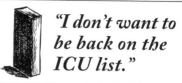 *"I don't want to be back on the ICU list."*
to get out of debt? Once your students go through the process of
getting caught up you will hear statements such as, "I don't want to
be back on the ICU list."

Winning the war on apathy/irresponsibility using the ICU list
is a process that works. It truly centers on putting the students first,
and teachers being empowered to help them. Are you and your staff
desperately trying to save your apathetic students? If so, then all staff
members must be trained in Academic CPR.

Chapter Nine

LIFEGUARDS REQUIRED

"At a swimming pool, a lifeguard has the responsibility of carefully watching over all of the swimmers. If at any time a swimmer looks in danger, a lifeguard will guide him back to a safe area. The lifeguard doesn't just leave it at that, but also encourages the swimmer to work hard on their swimming ability. Eventually, the lifeguard expects the swimmer to GET RESULTS on his own. Once the swimmer is confident with his swimming, the lifeguard continues to 'keep an eye' on the swimmer but will never leave him alone in the pool."

Stacy Bryant, 8th grade lifeguard at Southeast Middle School, Diamond, Ohio

In a Brick House, lifeguards are a required layer of daily support for teachers. No matter how large or small your school is you can provide the necessary set of eyes on a certain section of your student body. Some middle schools have sixth, seventh, and eighth grade lifeguards assigned to each grade level who work the list for one period of the day. Some high schools have several lifeguards just to make sure that no freshman academically drowns during that critical first year in high school. The number of lifeguards in a school is relative to the level of apathy, population, and floor plan of the school. Armed with the ICU list, lifeguards make daily contact like a doctor makes rounds to check on each patient with their assigned students and become invaluable to the teachers they support.

Matt Lacy, principal at Jackson Middle School, says this about Jason, their lifeguard: "While we haven't perfected ICU at JMS, we have jumped in with both feet this year and achieved some great things. I honestly don't think we would have been successful without our lifeguard. He does an excellent job and is a consistent presence that holds our students accountable. He talks to students, teachers and parents on a daily basis. Because he is so consistent, students understand that they have to complete the assignments and learn the material. He is most useful for those "extreme" students. He works constantly to figure out what interventions will work for different kids."

He talks to students, teachers and parents on a daily basis.

It does not matter how large or small your school is as long as you establish effective lifeguards to watch over individual sections of the student body on a daily basis.

At Southside, Arlene, an excellent para-professional covered over three hundred students in making her rounds every morning in about forty-five minutes. The students and teachers knew she was coming every day with the list. If they were on it, they had to respond with a plan of action. Occasionally a student would not respond which meant a meeting with the guidance counselor or principal. Our teachers thanked me over and over for assigning Arlene as another set of eyes on each student by working the ICU list every morning.

Southeast Middle School assistant principal, Mat Prezioso, believes that choosing the right person to be a lifeguard is extremely important. He says, "Lifeguards are a crucial element to our ICU. It is vital to get the right people in those roles. Folks who will get to know students and their individual situations. We have one lifeguard per grade level. They have one period per day to do their thing. Each grade has an 'intervention/mini class' period per day. This is where most of our re-teaching takes place. If a student is on the list they go to that teacher for that period. The lifeguards make sure they get there and help students get their assignments complete. They also form relationships with many students and know their stories. Our lifeguards are the all-stars of our building. All first round draft picks! Self-starters who do what is best for kids!"

South Gibson County High School has an excellent lifeguard who is a Special Education Assistant. She says it only takes her about twenty minutes right before lunch to update who did not show for extra help during ICU time. Students who missed ICU are called down during their lunch period by two other lifeguards. South Gibson closes all the cracks students try to slip through on a daily basis. As a result, one hundred percent of their freshmen passed to the tenth grade for the past two years!

Spring Oaks Middle in Houston, Texas has two extremely effective lifeguards. Every day they walk the halls with their IPADS (ICU list) and have conversations with students about their missing assignments during first period. I shadowed them one morning and this is what I observed:

1. Students did not have to be asked what they owed, they already knew.

2. All students were actively engaged in conversation about "their list".

3. Not one student even thought about not completing one of "their" assignments. They assumed they would get it done.

4. Every student knew the lifeguard would follow up the next day.

Administrators Must Make the Lifeguard Rounds

Brad Berens, principal at Mitchell Middle School, says, "As an administrator, I try to make the lifeguard rounds at the eighth grade level as often as I can. It helps me stay in touch with that part of ICU and, for some students, it helps to change up who is visiting with them." Brad says it is helpful to students to see the administrator involved and he recommends "doing the rounds" with the lifeguard once a week if possible. I loved this part of my job at Southside because I was in a secondary role simply listening to the discussion about missing assignments. My presence was usually all that was necessary for the student to feel a sense of urgency in getting their list cleaned up. Some of the toughest situations need to be handled by the principal so being in touch with the list is paramount in effectively dealing with the most apathetic students. Administrators, if you want to show your students you really care, and motivate your staff to keep working hard, hang out in the halls with your lifeguard as much as possible.

Guidance Counselors Must Make the Lifeguard Rounds

I recently received this question from an ICU lifeguard, "As you all know, the toughest students generally have the toughest lives. At this point of the year many of these students are telling me about personal issues and about their relationships with staff. How do I handle this?" My reply was simple: "Your guidance counselor should make the rounds with you as often as possible."

Lifeguards will experience a number of students who will want to share personal issues related to home life because it often relates to missing assignments. Sometimes students need to discuss relationship issues with some of their teachers, which can put a lifeguard in an uncomfortable position. Guidance counselors are trained to deal with relationship issues. I strongly recommend the guidance counselor go with the lifeguard at least once a week. This is what Linda, our counselor at Southside did because it was a proactive way for her to connect with students who needed her help. The lifeguards actually get to know the students better than anyone else and they develop wisdom and discernment in preventing student meltdowns.

Every Adult is a Lifeguard in a Brick House

Office Staff - During the summer, before the 2010-2011 school year, my secretary decided she was going to have the ICU list of missing assignments on her computer throughout the day. Parents/grandparents would routinely pick their child up early or check them out for lunch. During the three to five minute wait she would say to the parent, "By the way, were you aware that your child owes Mr. Presley problem set 51 in math?" Often, the student would be sent back to class by the parent and the assignment would be completed by the next day.

Often, the student would be sent back to class by the parent and the assignment would be completed by the next day.

At Southeast Middle School the secretary said, "I told a mom what her daughter owed the other day when she came to pick her up early. The mom asked me 'What's this list thing?' I explained it and she said, 'It's about time we did something like this!' Mom was fussing at her all the way to the car and the assignment was off the list the next day."

School Nurse - Southside's nurse started checking the ICU list before she checked the student's temperature. Sometimes, the fake "sick tummy" was a result of several missing assignments and the student would return to class not wanting mom notified.

Coaches - The coaches at South Gibson County High School routinely pull players out their first period class for 2-3 minutes to ask for an explanation and plan if any of their players ever appear on the ICU list. Of course, players are rarely on the list. Coaches who want to keep all of their players eligible will check the list daily.

Principal - I always referred to the ICU list after dealing with a discipline issue or any discussion in my office with a student. Before they left, I would always ask "Are you on the list?" It became routine and students would usually voluntarily respond, "I am

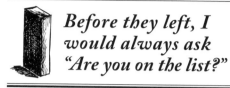

Before they left, I would always ask "Are you on the list?"

not on the list," or, "I do owe Mrs. Thompson a Social Studies assignment, Mr. Hill, but I am almost finished and will have it to her by the end of the day."

Band and choir members are held accountable to the ICU list by their director in most ICU schools. General questions like, "How are your grades?" and "Do you owe any work?" in the past allowed students to slip through the cracks. The days of communicating through our students are over because the list becomes the bottom line.

Cafeteria Staff - Have you ever thought about getting your cafeteria staff involved? A principal at one school recruited a few of the lunch ladies to question a few of his "tougher students" about missing assignments as they passed by in the lunch line. You never know who will be able to connect with a particular child.

Bus Drivers - Some bus drivers have excellent rapport with the students they drive each day. Certain drivers can be trusted to remind/question students about missing assignments.

Para Professionals - Always enlist your paraprofessionals into the army of support. At many ICU schools, these educational assistants are assigned specific students to monitor daily.

Counselors - Counselors discuss family and peer relationships with students throughout the school day. A simple, "Are you on the list?" should be the last question asked before a student leaves their office. If there is a missing assignment, the counselor should call the lifeguard or administrator to follow up.

Special Education teachers - A resource math teacher at one ICU school says, "I love the list because it is 'live' so my students cannot get by with 'I think I turned that in'." Another resource teacher says, "It keeps me in touch with all my students in their regular education classes so I can be proactive in making sure they stay caught up. We used to rely on the students' word and they always thought they were doing better than they really were."

Lifeguards are a back-up set of eyes

Let's say you take your 2-year-old and 4-year-old to the public swimming pool this summer. As they enter the pool, you look up and notice there is a lifeguard on duty. Since the lifeguard's job is to make sure nobody drowns, you think to yourself, "I think I will take a nap on the lounge chair while my children go for a swim." Absolutely not! Your eyes are on your children every second from the moment you enter the swimming area. Your children are your responsibility and the lifeguard is a back-up set of eyes. This is exactly the way it is supposed to work in a Brick House. Teachers should never put missing assignments on the ICU list and assume that it is the lifeguard's responsibility to get those assignments turned in. Lifeguards are a back-up set of eyes and teachers are the primary caretakers. How can any student

Lifeguards are a back-up set of eyes and teachers are the primary caretakers.

academically drown with so many lifeguards actively pulling for them to succeed?

Chapter Ten

A SHADOW OF A GRADE

"Why would anyone want to change current grading practices? The answer is quite simple: grades are so imprecise that they are almost meaningless."

– Dr. Robert Marzano

Friday night football between two rival schools becomes the focus of a "canned food drive competition." The local news media challenges both schools to bring in the most canned goods to support the Second Harvest Food Bank. The winner will be announced before the game on Friday night and the winning school will get recognized on the ten o'clock news. Both schools have been on the target list for having low graduation rates and need some positive press. A few overzealous teachers start giving academic points for bringing in beans. But what about the cheap brand of pork and beans; should they count the same as the more expensive Bush's Beans? The cheap brand tastes like cardboard but the Bush's and Van Camp's have brown sugar, real pieces of pork, and taste good. Taste should matter. Is it really fair to give the same amount of bonus points to all brands? Of course not, we must give more points for the expensive brand. Maybe the school board can untangle this mess.

Are you giving your students a grade or a shadow of a grade? Recall that in Plato's Allegory (Chapter 2) people watch shadows projected on the wall of the cave and believe the shadows are authentic because it is all they have ever known. Giving a student points for bringing in canned goods can be referred to as a shadow of a grade and is the result of false assumptions passed down within the teaching profession. Dr. Ken O'Connor, the Grade Doctor, says that in many secondary schools grades are broken and may actually harm students. In addition to Dr. O'Connor, and other grading experts agree that in order for a grade to be meaningful it must be a reflection of student learning.

In his book <u>Ahead of the Curve</u>, Dr. Reeves states, "Thanks to an abundance of research and documented practice, we know what to do." If our grades are meaningless but we know what to do, then what is the problem? Teachers can't seem to agree with

Teachers can't seem to agree with each other on what a grade should be.

each other on what a grade should be. However, in a Brick House, teachers refuse to give students a shadow of a grade and desire for grades to be meaningful. Just like a surveyor uses a plumb line to give them perfect vertical alignment, we must agree to align our grades with truth from the experts.

If a perfect grading policy existed, we would all be using it. Instead of chasing a perfect policy, soak yourself in these four truths and allow yourself time to digest and apply them. By applying these truths, you and your school will cultivate healthier grading practices that stimulate student engagement and hold students accountable for learning. Unhealthy grading practice is a contributing factor to student apathy.

TRUTH #1

"The purpose of a grade is to provide an accurate description of how well students have learned." - Dr. Thomas Guskey

To keep it simple, as you give a student a grade on a test, assignment, or report card ask yourself one question: How closely does this grade reflect what this student has learned? Giving academic points for bringing in canned goods has students chasing shadows and is part of a dysfunctional grading system. For your entertainment, I have accumulated a list of real items used by real teachers from across the country that reflect shadows in our thinking in relation to grades.

- A high school freshman had one month left in the school year and was passing every subject except one. She told me, "Mr. Hill, the only way I am going to pass English is if I clean the teacher's board more often, my teacher gives 20 bonus points to anyone who cleans her board." I suggested she clean the teacher's board every day thinking she might end up with an A. Discouraged, she said, "I can't because there is a waiting list to clean the board, my only chance to pass is if someone is absent and I get to fill in."

- Academic points for dry erase markers, paper towels, and other supplies are sometimes given because the school system does an inadequate job of supplying teachers with the resources they need.

- Dropping the lowest grade is a common practice in many classrooms.

- Some teachers give what they call easy 100s and tell students, "Just do the work and show it to me."

> *Dropping the lowest grade is a common practice in many classrooms.*

- Some teachers give folder grades for turning in a neat science or social studies folder.

- A teacher near Memphis thought he looked like Elvis Presley, so he gave points to students if they called him "Coach Elvis."

- One teacher loved Diet Dr. Pepper so he gave his students an A in PE if they brought him a 6 pack of Diet Dr. Pepper.

- A student was given a passing grade in English because he went to the teacher's house on the weekend and tilled the teacher's garden.

- A student was struggling in government class and the teacher made a deal with the student, "I have this horse that I really love and he needs to be put down but I don't have the heart to do it myself. I know you hunt. If you will shoot my horse for me, then I will make sure you pass government." He passed. (I think he was Valedictorian!)

And the list continues with deducting points:

- Minus 10 because you forgot to write your name
- Minus 10 points for each day late
- Minus all points because, "I don't take late work!"
- Minus points for behavior, effort, or responsibility

If any of this grading nonsense goes on in your school, your school culture reflects dysfunction. How can you ever expect to help students coming from dysfunctional families if your school culture is dysfunctional?

Are you Chasing Shadows with your grading patterns? If so, it will wear you out, confuse the students, and fuel apathy. In a Brick House grades reflect learning.

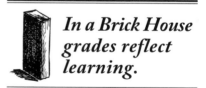

In a Brick House grades reflect learning.

TRUTH #2

"Inaccurate feedback is counter-productive." - Dr. Rick Stiggins

If the grades we put on tests, assignments, or report cards do not accurately reflect student learning, it hurts everyone. Dr. Rick Stiggins, founder and executive director of the ETS Assessment Training Institute, says he believes strongly that, "Assessment results must be accurate in all contexts. Inaccurate data leads to counterproductive instructional decisions, and thus it is harmful to students."

Consider the following examples:

Ryan turns in a perfect project in which he clearly shows he learned the standard being taught. However, the project was turned in late and his teacher's policy is to reduce the grade by several points. Because a grade is simply feedback and its sole purpose is to reflect learning, this is a skewed grade. As a teacher, are you sure you have a right to do this or are you chasing a shadow because it just feels right?

Amy is an over-achiever and will do anything to get a higher grade. She is not satisfied with a 100%, 103% is better, and 105% is best. Her teacher gives extra points for paper towels and dry erase markers because she has to pay for these supplies out of her own pocket. Amy brings in enough paper towels and dry erase markers to get a 105%

The problem: her grades reflected her over-achieving personality and tenacious work ethic.

every grading period. She has a GPA of 4.0 which is the highest she can possibly achieve in her district. She is valedictorian but scores 18 on the math portion of her ACT which means she must take a "non-credit" remedial math course her freshman year of college. The problem: her grades reflected her over-achieving personality and tenacious work ethic. Her grades have been a false reflection of learning and as Stiggins points out, this is "inaccurate feedback" and "harmful." This is the type of false information colleges and universities continue to criticize.

Emily is extremely apathetic so she starts to fall behind. Her teachers have pacing guides to follow so they feel pressure to move on. She is from a very dysfunctional family and hopelessness has been wearing her down since fourth grade. She is now in the eighth grade and her teachers allow her to sit in class and do nothing saying, "She is old enough to choose if she wants to pass or not." Her grades are all below 40%. In the middle of the second semester, Emily is placed in her district's alternative school. The culture change is good for her because teachers at her new school hold her accountable for learning the standards. Her grades improve and her achievement test scores show proficiency in every subject; however, the district policy says that all grades must be AVERAGED. Her first semester grades are so low that her final averages are all below passing. Even though Emily just finished the year with her best academic success, based on school board policy she still must repeat the eighth grade

Dr. Doug Reeves, in his 2008 keynote address at the Assessment and Evaluation Symposium, clearly explains that averaging a student's grades

"...averaging a student's grades is a toxic grading practice because it results in inaccurate feedback."

is a toxic grading practice because it results in inaccurate feedback. Since many of our apathetic students come from "toxic living conditions," we must provide them with a healthy school culture.

Truth in grading will set you free from giving students a shadow of a grade because, as Dr. O'Connor says, "Faulty grading damages students (and teachers)." Stop sending home false information, embrace the standards, and move as quickly as you can toward healthy grading practice in your daily decisions.

TRUTH #3

Learning is not a race or a competition.

"Our traditional grading culture encourages competition rather than collaboration, point accumulation rather than learning, and activities rather than results," according to Dr. O'Connor. Is learning supposed to be a competition? The truth is that learning is a process not a race and many students are shutting down because they do not want to compete. Top students and some of their parents love to try to make learning a race because it gives them a sense of superiority. Pacing guides are a new pressure our teachers feel as a result of standards-based curriculum. "Benchmarking" our students frequently is another routine that says to teachers, "Keep pace and speed up. You are moving too slowly." Pacing guides and benchmark assessments can be a very healthy practice as long as teachers do not allow learning to become a race for our children.

Kindergarten teachers follow pacing guides and benchmark each student but find a way to protect the learning process. Several years ago at my school we had twin girls enter kindergarten who had invented their own language. This "private language" is called Cryptophasia, or *twin talk*. (It sounded like gibberish.) While they completely understood each other they could not communicate with anyone else. My fabulous kindergarten teacher, Linda Davidson, found a way for these girls to engage in the learning process. Here is part of her story:

"I learned right away that they loved to play house so we taught them colors and letters in a playhouse setting. I used Play-Doh to make letters because the girls thought they were making cookies. Once they learned their letters and most of their sounds, they started talking to the other students. Although they were way behind the other students, they never lost interest and learned enough of the academic standards at a proficient level to move on to first grade."

Although these girls were seriously behind when they entered kindergarten, they were met by an outstanding team of educators including para-professionals, a speech pathologist, and several teachers who tenaciously engaged them in the learning process. Several of the twin's classmates entered school already reading but Linda followed her pacing guide, challenged every child, and the twins had a successful year. (The twins were never retained and graduated from high school last year!)

"But in HIGH SCHOOL we teach concepts that build upon one another," is a comment I hear frequently from secondary teachers who try to rationalize why they leave students behind. When kindergarten teachers are in my presentation along with secondary teachers, the kindergarten teachers bristle at that comment. The statement implies this problem is exclusive to secondary. While interviewing Linda Davidson about our twin girls, I also asked her to respond to, "But in HIGH SCHOOL we teach concepts that build upon one another." She immediately burst out laughing and sarcastically said, "Oh WOW, that's a new thing. We've never heard that before." If you think the range of student abilities is wider in secondary than it is in the primary grades, shadow a kindergarten teacher for a week and your thinking will change. Linda somehow connected with the girls and found a way to teach them to recognize all twenty six letters. She used all of her resources to teach them the sound each letter makes (just the letter A would wear me out), then provided lots of extra help so they could put together the sounds to recognize and speak words. She did all of this by using every minute of the school day providing each child the extra time and help they needed.

Teachers are faced with the same challenge in every grade level. I taught eighth and ninth grade science for ten years, was an assistant principal at a large high school for four years, and principal of a kindergarten through eighth grade school for twenty years. In my experience, primary teachers generally believe it is their job to meet the student where they are and engage them in the learning process while many secondary teachers believe it is the student's "responsibility" to meet the teacher where they are and stay caught up. Excellent teachers at all levels of education find a way to meet every child where they are, engage them in the learning process, and keep a healthy pace in teaching the academic standards. Our children must have excellent teachers in every subject and in every grade level.

What about rewarding speed in your grading system? Should students who learn a standard faster make a higher grade? I hear this statement frequently from teachers: "The students who study hard and do well the first time should get a higher grade." I must admit this does sound good and just seems right but it is a shadow in our thinking because grades must reflect student learning, not speed. According to Thomas Guskey, "To become an integral part of the instructional process, assessments cannot be a one shot, 'do or die' experience for students. Instead, assessments must be part of an ongoing effort to help students learn." In a Brick House, grades reflect learning, inaccurate feedback is counter-productive, and learning is not a race.

> ### *In a Brick House, grades reflect learning, inaccurate feedback is counter-productive, and learning is not a race.*

TRUTH #4

"Honor learning." – Ken O'Connor, The Grade Doctor

Learning cannot be secondary. Many will say that student learning comes first, but rarely implement practices that reflect this principle. *Honor* means great respect is given because of worth or high rank. In your school, is *learning* clearly ranked higher than everything else?

Most educators are taught to establish their classroom rules and routines at the beginning of school which is important. However, learn the *rules and routines* must not drown out *learn the standards*. What if every teacher on the first day of school within the first ten minutes pointed to the academic standards, posted on the classroom walls (in student friendly language), and stated, "This is what we are going to *learn* together this year. Look around the room for a few minutes, try to find something that you might already know something about," then facilitate a discussion using the word *learn* throughout. In reflecting on my ten years as a secondary science teacher, it is embarrassing to admit that I possibly never used the word *learn*. We had *establish good classroom management* drilled into us, so that is pretty much all we talked about with our students the first few weeks.

I also remember making statements like, "This is important because it will be on your next test." My students did not *honor learning* because I did not give it the highest rank in importance. And, with all of the emphasis on achievement test scores, teachers must fight the urge to say, "This is important because it will be on your achievement test."

Does the culture of your school give a higher rank to grades or learning? Most schools have an "Honor Roll" which is posted in the local newspaper. Parents love their bumper stickers with, "My child is an Honor Roll student." If grades are not a true reflection of student learning, then why do we honor grades with an "Honor Roll?" One of my primary grade teachers explained the kindergarten culture like this, "We eat, drink, and breathe academic standards all day every day." "What did you learn today," is a question parents and teachers soak children in throughout the primary grades. When a child reaches fourth grade, teachers, parents, and other adults begin to soak students in, "How are your grades?" and "What did you get on that test?" which dishonors learning.

According to my wife, Debbie, who has been a high school teacher, counselor, and graduation coach for twenty eight years, "Many of the most highly motivated high school students choose classes they have no interest in because they will earn more points contributing to their grade point average and therefore rank. It is a strategic and unfortunate game." Does *accumulating points* and *making good grades* rank higher than *learning the standards* in your school culture? **Honor learning!**

Chapter Eleven

PANDEMONIUM HIGH SCHOOL

Pandemonium is the opposite of harmony but both terms can be used to describe culture. Dr. Lynn Canady, a leading educational consultant and researcher, uses a baseball field as an analogy to describe the wide range of children that enter our schools each year. He says that children who have great homes enter the classroom already on third base. All the teacher has to do is move them from third base to home plate. Some children come in from second base, generally due to the chaos and dysfunction in their family, which means that their teachers will have to move them twice as far to get them home. Other students start on first base making it a far greater challenge for teachers to get them home. Actually we have too many children, like the twins, who are in the dugout and have no clue there is a game going on, but we are still expected to teach them. Canady also says that half of the dropouts used to do their work but had something like a tragedy, divorce, or significant change in the family that got them off track and the pandemonium in their lives caused them to shut down. He says that most schools are not equipped to re-direct these students so they dropout. What about your school?

Pandemonium High School represents a traditional school culture in which each teacher has generated their own grading policy and isolation among the teachers is the norm. The accepted teacher paradigm is, "*I* teach *my* subject to my students. Students are old enough now to keep up with what *I* expect out of them and grades will come from a number of items *I* believe to be important." Many students become confused as they travel from teacher to teacher trying to keep up with the wide variety of points, daily grades, test grades, project grades, bonus points, extra credit, and point deductions.

David represents one of your students whose life has been turned upside down. He and his three younger sisters just moved in with their grandmother who lives in the Pandemonium school zone. Their mother has just started serving her one-year prison sentence. All four children are upset with her because they had to leave all of their friends at their old school. They are also worried about mom's safety. David is entering his critical freshman year of high school and the recent significant change in his life has him off track. Since teachers at PHS have never discussed, studied, or learned about healthy grading practices, David will be exposed to pandemonium in grading. Let's follow him as he tries to figure out each of his eight teachers.

1st Period

Science – Mr. Mayhem explains that he takes one grade per day for daily grades based on daily work, effort, being on time, behavior, and having all of your supplies. Tests will be given every Friday and will count double. Daily grades will count 50% and test grades 50%. No gum, water, or restroom breaks unless you have an emergency. David raises his hand and asks, if I have to use the restroom, does that count off from my grade?

2nd Period

Math – Mr. Bedlam hands out an explanation of how he grades and tells students that it is their responsibility to read the handout and keep it in there math folder so they can always have a copy of how grades will be figured in his room. "You are high school students now, so you are old enough to be able to keep up with my policy yourselves. I am trying to prepare you for the real world."

The handout explains that daily work/homework counts 40% of their math grade and tests count 60%. Homework will be given every night and checked the next day. Tests will be given at the end of each chapter. Water is permitted and there is a restroom pass on my desk if you need to go. You must sign your name on the restroom form and the time you leave and then return the pass and write in the time you return. A student asks, "If I bring a package of water for you will you give me bonus points" I don't do well on tests."

3rd Period

English – Mrs. Orderly spends the first two days explaining her grading "policy" so there will be no confusion on how "she" grades. "Vocabulary tests will be given every Friday and will count for 20% of your grade, homework will be given three times per week and it will count for 30% of your grade, there will be a writing project every grading period and it will count for 30%, and tests will be given every two weeks and they will count for 20%. By now, all of the students who did not start on third base are getting a knot in their stomach thinking, "I am soooooo confused and I really wanted to do better this year!"

4th Period

Spanish – Mrs. Chaos says, "Everything counts in here from the moment you walk in the door until you leave. I will grade your attitude, behavior, effort, tests, daily work, homework, and projects. Everything counts and everything will be averaged into your grade. I do not take late work, this is not junior high, and you are old enough now to get your work in on time. If you don't pay your electric bill on time, they will cut off your electricity. I am trying to teach you responsibility and it would hurt you if I allowed you to turn anything in after my deadline." A student raises her hand and asks, "Did you say we would have points deducted if our parents were late paying their electric bill?"

5th Period through 8th Period

It doesn't matter because David is so overwhelmed and hopeless that he and a number of other students have returned to the dugout and are refusing to play the game.

"Figure out your teachers, son, because every teacher wants something different from you. You need to figure out what it is and then give it to them. This will help your grades." This is the advice I gave my son, Zach, before his freshman year of high school. It was the exact same advice his two older sisters and mother gave him. I call this the *game of school* and I was reluctantly advising him to *learn the game of school* so he could *make good grades*. The simple advice I had given him before entering kindergarten to *listen and learn* had deteriorated into *learn the game of school*. While many students are very good at playing the *game of school*, too many of our students are ill equipped to *play*.

The main problem with Pandemonium High School is that it is based on a false assumption that education is about the teacher instead of the students. "*I* teach *my* subject to *my* students. Students are old enough now to keep up with what *I* expect out of them and grades will come from a number of items *I* believe to be important."

 "Students are old enough now," is a reckless way of thinking and contributes to our student apathy problem.

The error in thought is, "It is all about me." The correct thought is, "It is not about you, it has never been about you, and it is never going to be about you." (Power of ICU) Education will always be about the student and student learning. "Students are old enough now," is a reckless way of thinking and contributes to our student apathy problem. What if you had eight different bosses to answer to every day? Each boss is isolated from the other and there is no harmony or continuity between the eight. What if each of your eight bosses generated their own expectations with eight different ways for you to earn your pay? Are you "old enough now" to keep up with all eight of your bosses' individual requirements? Would the chaos and confusion cause you to shut down?

> *"Can you imagine an orchestra with an "IT's all about me" outlook? Each artist clamoring for self-expression. Tubas blasting nonstop. Percussionists pounding to get attention. The cellist shoving the flutist out of the center-stage chair. The trumpeter standing atop the conductor's stool tooting his horn. Sheet music disregarded. Conductor ignored. What do you have but an endless tune-up session! Harmony? Hardly."*
>
> *(Max Lucado, <u>It's Not About Me</u>)*

Although each musician might be very talented, the lack of synchronization produces mayhem. Does this describe the way you and your staff "do grades?" If so, stop complaining about the students because your grading practices are a mess.

Chapter Twelve

HARMONY IN GRADING PRACTICE

Pandemonium High School reflects the same fragmented approach to grading we had at Southside before we started discussing and learning from the experts. As the truth permeated through our thinking, harmony replaced chaos as teachers made healthy changes to their grading practices on their own. I never told our teachers they had to change their grading policies. I never forced "no zeros" down their throats. The reason I share the four truths is because they are the main concepts which helped synchronize our grading. For example, since the purpose of a grade is to reflect what a student has learned, teachers started asking themselves, "What does this grade reflect?" Although teachers maintained a certain amount of subjectivity, we drastically reduced the pandemonium for our students with the following healthy grading guidelines:

Students Never Heard
- Bonus points for supplies
- Point deductions
- Easy 100's
- Drop the lowest grade

Students Consistently Heard
- Your grades will reflect what you have learned
- You must show me you learned the standard
- Improve your learning level and your grade will improve
- I will provide whatever help you need

Students Experienced Harmony in Grade Books

Audrey Harrington, Southside Middle School math teacher, introduced the concept of using a standards based grade book to our entire staff. We decided to use that school year to study and share the new concept before making the transition to standards based grade books for all teachers. Allowing a full year for the changeover proved to be a wise decision which resulted in full teacher buy-in for the next year. Our traditional grade books with chapter tests grades and daily grades had been replaced with the individual learning standards. This created vertical consistency for our students as they progressed to the next grade level and horizontal consistency in middle school while moving from class to class. In fact, we had some students who noticed that grading in the

 Our traditional grade books... had been replaced with the individual learning standards.

upper grades was a lot like the way they did things in kindergarten.

Students Heard Harmony in Learning Levels

For years we had noticed a lack of correlation between our students' grades and their achievement scores. Every year we had too many students who made As and Bs on their report cards but could not pass the achievement test. We also had a few students who made Ds and Fs but would do very well on the achievement test. Since Tennessee uses the terms **Advanced, Proficient, Basic, and Below Basic** to report student learning levels, we decided it would help our students and their parents if we used the same terminology on a daily basis. On every whiteboard in every classroom students saw these four learning levels. Teachers would refer to these four terms while giving feedback to students. For example, on a ten question assessment over multiplying decimals, the student would receive a ratio with the number correct over the total number of questions. This was a very simple way for students to find their learning level on the whiteboard because the teacher correlated the number correct with the level of learning.

Number Correct	Learning Level
10	Advanced
8,9	Proficient
6,7	Basic
0-5	Below Basic

Instead of writing the learning level on the students' papers, teachers always asked, "What is your learning level?" And, since students were required to find their own learning level, it helped to engage them in the learning process which motivated them to improve. Upon receiving test results, students started making statements like, "YES! I finally made it to proficient," and, "Oh man, if I had gotten one more right, I would have been proficient." Using Advanced, Proficient, Basic, and Below Basic as common language helped eradicate the game of school from our culture. Instead of discussing grades first, our parents started focusing on their child's learning and teachers began moving toward grades that more accurately reflected student learning. In Ken O'Connor's book, How to Grade for Learning, he says, "First and foremost, the teacher must stop thinking in terms of assignments, tests, and activities to which points are assigned, and start thinking in terms of levels of performance." (O'Connor 2002, pp. 147, 150)

Another Fine Mess

Here's Another Fine Mess You've Gotten Me Into is the title of a 1930's movie starring the comedy team Laurel and Hardy. Oliver Hardy made the catchphrase, "Another fine mess," famous as Stan Laurel, his clumsy partner, repeatedly created chaos for the two in comedy sketches and movies. Haven't teachers been handed "another fine mess" to clean up? They are given a set of standards to teach but report cards remain traditional, "Because the parents are not ready for a standards based report card." Achievement test scores use learning levels for each standard but report cards still only allow for a single number grade. Will report cards ever change to reflect the standards students are supposed to learn? Instead of waiting to find out, take control of the things you can control and simplify as much as possible.

Suggested guidelines:

- Challenging every student to "Move Up" to the next learning level can be used as the motivator because as stated earlier, "Research indicates that moving closer to achieving a goal triggers a part of the brain linked to motivation."
- All four learning levels are written on the board in every classroom.
- All scores are given in a ratio which correlates with a learning level on the board. Teachers will have numbers they can use for report cards. There is no perfect way to do this but grades will end up being a better reflection of learning than traditional grades which according to Dr. Robert Marzano have become "meaningless."
- All teachers refer to the learning levels in their daily language, but students must know their learning level on each standard. Before the ICU list students did not know what they owed. With the list, students are able to tell you exactly what they owe. Now, hold students accountable and responsible for knowing their learning levels. And, remember, there is power in a list.

Because there is so much pressure on teachers to push students to the proficiency level, many have resorted to challenging everyone to be "proficient." However, telling a student who is below basic that their goal is to become proficient does not motivate nearly as much as to simply challenge him to **move up** to the next level. Basic is the next step and one step at a time makes the goal reachable (Dave Ramsey approach). Is it possible for top students to be satisfied with proficiency if that is all they ever hear? Emphasizing the term "proficiency" might demotivate them from continuing to push towards being advanced on every standard.

Student Friendly and Simple Conversation

The students will transition smoothly to this approach if you let them discuss their favorite video games. When you ask, "What is the goal of your favorite game?" many will say something like, "To master a level and then **move up** to the next level." They will probably tell you that it takes lots of practice to advance to another point. Using their approach to video games, simply tell them to apply the same concept with the academic

They will probably tell you that it takes lots of practice to advance to another point.

standards. Mastering the next learning level on a specific standard can be a motivator for students and build an intrinsic sense of accomplishment which many of our children are lacking.

Student A

Teacher: What is your learning level on order of operation?

Student A: I am proficient on order of operation.

Teacher: What is your goal?

Student A: To **move up** to advanced.

Teacher: What do you need to **move up**?

Student A: Extra practice.

Teacher offers several extra practice options then says:

Show me you are ready to **move up**.

Student B

Teacher: What is your learning level on order of operation?

Student B: I am below basic on order of operation.

Teacher: What is your goal?

Student B: To **move up** to basic.

Teacher: What do you need to **move up**?

Student B: Extra practice.

Teacher offers several extra practice options then says:

Show me you are ready to **move up**.

All students are challenged using student friendly language. Instead of the teacher feeling pressure to reteach everything to everybody, peer tutoring and use of technology will become commonly used resources for extra practice. If you ask your students, "How can you get extra practice?" and all they say is "From my teacher," then you know you do not have a full menu of extra practice provided. And, keeping in mind that you have been handed "another fine mess" to clean up, apply the four grading truths discussed in Chapter 10 as guidelines for determining grades.

1. Move toward grades being a healthy reflection of what students have learned.

2. Inaccurate feedback is counter-productive.

3. Move away from making grades a competition and stop rewarding speed.

4. Focusing on learning levels for each standard.

Always apply what you learned from the bill collectors (apathy experts) and financial advisors (responsibility experts) when "helplessness" tries to discourage you with thoughts like, "But what do I do if…?" The answer is always the same: Use a list, check off what has been learned, and never leave them alone.

 Use a list, check off what has been learned, and never leave them alone.

Outstanding teachers will discern the game of school from learning. When Jackson Middle School in Jackson, Missouri was in their first year of building a Brick House, I received the following email. Sarah Reinecke, seventh grade language arts teacher, was reflecting on a conference she had attended where she experienced common pandemonium in grading.

At one of my sessions, some teachers were asking a presenter, "Well, how do you grade that?" The presenter responded without a definite answer. Others chimed in as to how many points note-taking would be worth. Debate begins as the grading ball is volleyed back and forth. "Forty-five points!" "Oh, that is way too many." "I'd give it at least 20 points."

I had to smile. I don't live in that world anymore. All those teachers were freaking out over points. Not me. I freak out over learning. It has taken some time to get there, and after listening to that conversation, I've realized what a shift I've made! I left that session KNOWING we got a good thing going at JMS!

How many points should note-taking be worth? Is forty five too many? Is twenty points enough? Because the JMS staff started having discussions on healthy grading practices at the beginning of the school year, Sarah was able to discern the main purpose, student learning, from the shadow of point accumulation. She references the game of school when she says, "Debate begins as the grading ball is volleyed back and forth." Make healthy grading practice your focus. Students will stop hearing the "points" game and they will start hearing, "Your grade will be a reflection of what you have learned."

Chapter Thirteen

TOP OF THE MIND

In the 1991 movie *City Slickers*, Mitch (Billy Crystal) is a middle aged, successful, big-city salesman having a mid-life crisis. He and his two friends, Ed and Phil, go on a cattle drive vacation seeking their true purpose in life. Throughout the movie, the tough trail boss, Curly, repeatedly asks Mitch a simple question. "You know what life is? One thing." Mitch continued to respond, "What? What is the one thing?" And Curly would repeatedly say, "When you find it, you'll know." This drove Mitch crazy until he and his friends found renewal and purpose through their experiences on the cattle drive. At the end of the movie Mitch could clearly define his "one thing." In John Miller's book <u>Outstanding: 47 Ways to Make Your Organization Exceptional</u>, he explains the importance of clearly defining the "one thing" or main purpose in order for any organization to be "outstanding." In addition to clearly defining the "one thing," Miller teaches that it must be on the top of every stakeholder's mind every minute of every day. In chapter three, *Keep the Mission "Top of the Mind"*, he states, "For some organizations there is no doubt about why they exist. It's as if the word "mission" is built right into their name…In an outstanding organization, the mission is always on top of mind."

Have you clearly defined that "one thing" at your school? If you individually ask teachers, parents, students, and para-professionals, "What is the main reason we all come to school every day?" Will the answers be the same? My nephew, Taylor Hill, is a very successful baseball player. He pitched for Vanderbilt University for four years and is presently pitching professionally in the minor leagues for the Washington Nationals. I recently asked Taylor, "What is the main thing your pitching coach preaches to you and the other pitchers?" He is always consistent and emphatic with his answer, "Pound the strike zone, Uncle Danny, if I do not throw strikes, then my team has no chance of winning. A pitcher's main purpose is to throw strikes!" Taylor says that before every pitch he has, "Pound the strike zone," on the top of his mind.

After reading *Top of the Mind* several times as a principal, I realized that all stakeholders at Southside could not answer the critical question, "Why do we come to school every day?" Like most schools, we had a mission statement that used acceptable educational catch phrases like, "Develop students into responsible citizens," and, "Teach students to be life-long learners." We posted our mission statement in our hallways and checked off all of the state and local requirements but it was not on the top of everyone's mind every day. Since it did not use student friendly terminology and was too complex, it was basically worthless. Can any student tell you what

> *Since it did not use student friendly terminology and was too complex, it was basically worthless.*

your school mission statement is? During presentations I often ask if any teacher or administrator knows their school mission statement and the common response is a vigorous "NO" along with lots of laughter. The only teachers on my staff who could quote our mission statement were the ones on our school improvement committee in charge of that section of our school improvement plan. Although we had a great school and students were completing every assignment, based on Miller's criteria, Southside was not an outstanding organization. Our main purpose was not clearly defined nor was it on the *top of everybody's mind every day.*

At the beginning of the 2010-11 school year, I decided to get on the intercom and attempt to nail down *Top of the Mind.* Could we immerse our school culture in honoring learning the academic standards? I was going to make sure every staff member, parent, and student knew why we came to Southside every day. Here is what I said:

> *Teachers, get your favorite color dry erase marker and find an area of your whiteboard that is clearly visible to everyone. I want to make sure everyone at Southside knows for sure the main reason we come to school every day. Teachers I want you to write the following guidelines on your board and refer to them throughout the school year.*
>
> *Number one -* **Learn the Standards.** *The main reason we come to school every day is to make sure you, the students, learn the standards. Teachers, please write next to number one, Learn the Standards. Students you already know what the standards are because your teacher has them written on the walls of your classroom and tells you which standard is being covered daily. The main reason we all come to Southside every single day is to make sure that you, our students, learn the standards.*
>
> *Number two -* **91.** *Teachers, write the number ninety-one on your board next to number two. Students, we have ninety-one adults that come to Southside every day with one main purpose and that is to make sure that you, our students, learn the standards.*
>
> *Number three -* **Tell Someone.** *Students, the main reason we come to school every day is to make sure that you, our students, learn the standards. If you have not learned something and need extra help you have to tell someone. Students, Southside*

has ninety-one adults for you to choose from but you have to tell someone. It does not matter how many times the teacher has covered it, if you still have not learned a standard, then you must tell someone. If your favorite teacher is your PE teacher, then tell her you need help with whatever the standard is. If your favorite person in the school is the librarian, then tell the librarian. You must tell someone that you need extra help. And students, just between you and me, if you ever tell any of my staff members that you need extra help and they do not get you the help you need, then you come tell me. Because the only reason we all come to school every day is to make sure that you, our students, learn the standards. If any of the adults think that something else is more important, then they have it wrong and we may need to have a chat.

*Number four - **Don't Fake It**. Students, most of you know that I had a bike wreck when I was young and lost the hearing in my left ear. Do you know that I only hear about half of what people say? Do you know that I say "HUH?" a lot and get embarrassed even as an adult when I still don't understand what was said? Because I become embarrassed as I see people getting frustrated having to repeat themselves, I usually end up nodding my head and faking it – acting like I hear them so we can move on. Students, some of you get embarrassed when the teacher covers something several times and it still does not click. Number four is don't fake it. Do not get embarrassed if you take longer to learn something and do not act like you have learned something if you really haven't.*

*Number five – **Extra Practice**. If you have not learned a standard, you must tell someone you need help. You have ninety-one adults to choose from. You cannot fake it, and we will be happy to give you extra practice on whatever standard you have not learned. In basketball, if a player isn't a good dribbler, the coach tells them they need more practice. If a member of*

the band is playing his instrument off key, the band director
simply says, "You need extra practice." Students, there is
nothing wrong with needing extra practice because the only
reason we all come to school every day is to make sure that all
of you learn the standards.

That first announcement took about fifteen minutes and the whole
school was very quiet. I had several of my teachers thank me for
"simplifying things."

I reminded everyone of the five guidelines a couple more
times over the next few weeks in the hope that it would take root.
A few months later we had visitors from an Alabama school that
wanted to study our ICU. I took them to a seventh grade math
inclusion class and let them ask the students whatever they wanted.

 **I reminded everyone of the five guidelines
a couple more times over the next few
weeks in the hope that it would take root.**

Immediately, the first question was, "How many of you did not have
your assignment for today?" As usual, the students looked at me
as if to ask, "What are they talking about?" (Our students did not
view assignment completion as optional.) When all of our visitors'
questions were satisfied, I decided to question my students to see if
our main purpose was on the top of their minds.

Me: What is the main reason we come to school every day?
Students, loud and clear: To *learn the standards.*
Me: And how many…(they cut me off.)
Students: Ninety one!
Me: And if you haven't learned…(they cut me off again.)
Students: Tell someone, Mr. Hill, you have to tell someone!
Me: And you can't…
Students: Fake it, you can't fake it.

Me: What does that mean? What does, "You can't fake it," mean?
Several hands went up. One child answered: You can't act like you
learned it when you really haven't.
Me: And what are we going to do for you if you tell us you have
not learned a standard?
Students: Extra practice!
Me: Give me some examples of extra practice?
Lots of hands go up: We get extra practice on the computer using
Compass Learning and *Study Island*. (Educational software) We
can get extra help before school or after school in tutoring. I get
extra help in math lab during school. I struggle with reading and
my reading lab really helps me. And some of us have a peer tutor
for certain subjects.

I was pretty pumped so I decided to take the visitors with me to
the Wetlands. (This is what I called the kindergarten area because
the boys hands were always wet, the restroom walls and floors were
wet, and their faces seemed to always be wet.) There were about
fifteen kindergarten boys in line when I approached. "Freeze," I
said and they did.

Me: What is the main reason we come to Southside every day?
Five year old boys in unison: To *learn the standards.*
Me: And how many adults do we have at Southside to help you
learn the standards?
Five year old Boys: Ninety-one! (They were shouting.)
Me: And what do you have to do…(they cut me off.)
Five year old Boys: Tell somebody!

Most of them remembered don't fake it, and all of them remembered
extra practice.

What is the main purpose
of your school? Is it point
accumulation and competition or
student learning? If you do not

What is the main purpose of your school?

have a clearly stated main purpose that is on the top of everyone's mind every day, then chaos and dysfunction is your culture of choice. If the five year old kindergarten boys at Southside had the main purpose on the top of their minds, then it can be an attainable and measurable goal for every school.

Chapter Fourteen

But My Plate Is Full!

*"It is not hard to learn more. What is hard is
to unlearn when you discover yourself wrong."*
– Martin H. Fisher

If you try to "add" keeping a list of missing assignments to what you are already doing, then you will be "buried alive." Hoarding is the compulsion to accumulate and store large quantities of nonessential things. Hoarders cannot throw anything away. A popular television show, *Hoarders – Buried Alive*, tells the stories of hoarders struggling with behavior that has made every day existence unbearable for both them and their loved ones. Being a hoarder has nothing to do with intelligence, wealth, or occupation but requires a paradigm shift in order to remove nonessential items. Teachers who say, "But my plate is full," must examine what is on their plate.

Remove nonessentials that require a lot of time and energy.

Large Quantities of Grades

When research shows that grading every little thing does not improve learning, teachers generally respond: **"If I don't grade it, then they won't do it."**

If you believe in this shadow, then you are allowing your students to hold you hostage and dictate your workload. "My students imply to me that I have to grade it or else they won't do it, so I have to. They make me grade it." Who is in charge? Students should not be able to dictate your workload, and grading every little thing takes a tremendous amount of work on your part. Take this off your plate.

When I taught science, I always gave students the questions at the end of the chapter for a grade. I graded notebooks, worksheets, and study guides. I had six classes, two hundred forty students, and I thought I had to grade every little thing. What was I thinking? I wish someone would have given me permission to stop. I wish someone had pointed out to me the nonessential practices that wore me out and had no effect on student learning. The routine of many teachers includes giving ineffective worksheets, grading notebooks, and homework for a grade even though this reflects effort instead of learning. I hear from math teachers that feel overwhelmed by the ICU list, but they cannot stop giving a zillion math problems every night because that is *the way it has always been done.* One high school foreign language teacher buries her students with, "I grade everything!" She gives over one hundred and fifty grades per semester class and failures are rampant.

Rick Wormeli, award winning author and national speaker, says, "Grades are not compensation (you do that, I'll give you this) they are communication. Change the metaphor and paradigm." When you and your students stop viewing grades as compensation, you are able to shift your time and energy to improve the quality of each grade. By removing the large quantity of grades from your plate there will be plenty of room for essential practices such as checking for *Grades are not compensation...they are communication.* understanding and providing extra practice when needed. Then, requiring students to restudy and retake tests on material they did not learn becomes vital.

Insignificant Assignments

Some teachers bury their students alive with mass quantities of "work" because they have a compulsion to keep their students busy. A high school and its middle school feeder started ICU a year ago. The middle school teachers let go of nonessential practices, improved the quality of their assignments, and are moving toward giving grades that are a better reflection of learning. The middle school teachers removed ineffective and time-consuming items from their plates and replaced them with keeping an ICU list of assignments directly tied to the academic learning standards. Student engagement has improved dramatically in the middle school.

However, the high school teachers viewed the ICU list as an "additional thing to do" and continued to complain about having too much on their plate. Student apathy is still rampant and teachers are "buried alive" - unable to let go of bad teaching practices. A frustrated administrator summed it up: "Many of the high school teachers think we are adding on to our old house. They cannot seem to understand that we are building a new one." During a keynote speech recently, Dr. Rick Stiggins challenged teachers with this question: "What percent of the time do students do work for compliance to get a grade?" Assignments must hold the academic learning standard still and be practice for learning. Keeping a list of missing assignments...a list of "significant" missing assignments is an essential practice that never lets students off the hook for learning.

Hopelessness and Helplessness

One episode of *Hoarding - Buried Alive* examines a teacher who continues to accumulate women's shoes in her house. As her husband and teenage son showed the reporter the inside of their home, they had to move shoes in every room in order to clear a path to walk. The son was extremely distraught saying, "I have no room for myself and I can never invite my friends over because this is so embarrassing." Hoarders make every day existence unbearable for both themselves and their loved ones.

"What are we supposed to do about all the standards?"

"These pacing guides are impossible to follow."

Everyone within hearing range is exposed to their *helplessness*.

"We don't have enough time to teach all of this. They keep changing everything and expecting more and more out of us. Why should I even try?"

Hopelessness that is repeated daily.

Take control of the things you can control and stop whining about things out of your control. We all know the standards will probably change and supposedly "improve" every few years. We all know the state and federal officials will continue to expect more and more from us. Is this ok? Of course not, but if you have a compulsion to complain about it all the time, then move on to another profession. Sadly, some educators are hoarders of negative comments and make every day existence for fellow staff members unbearable.

Stubbornness

I run into teacher hoarders all the time who are just plain stubborn. They refuse to examine their plate and have decided to just keep doing what they have been doing for years, actively working against anything that resembles change. Dr. Doug Reeves says, "Too frequently, improvements in teaching and leadership are stopped cold by the cynical demand, 'Show me the proof that this will work!' Demands for perfect proof are nothing but smoke screens designed to prevent change."

Clean Your Plate and Start Over

Put only the essentials on your new plate. Our students come first. It is encouraging to see that most teachers refuse to listen to the hoarders. In a Brick House, hoarders are not allowed because they will bury your school with nonessential assignments, mass quantities of insignificant grades, and hopelessness. It is essential that student grades reflect *learning*. It is essential that we stop letting students off the hook for *learning*. And, it is essential that our assignments become *practice for learning*.

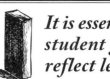

It is essential that student grades reflect learning.

Chapter Fifteen

Every Minute Counts

I often return for a follow up visit several months after starting ICU with a school. I love the opportunity to spend the day with the students and staff and provide suggestions for improvement. The follow up visit starts when the first student arrives on campus. I am mainly looking for extra time for students to complete missing assignment without losing valuable class time. I love this part of my job because it is easy to find down time and when I do it motivates the staff. In a recent follow up visit, for example, we discovered up to three hundred minutes of down time per week that was being wasted. Working with the leadership team, we quickly had a plan that would turn these lost minutes into minutes that count for academics. We were just getting started! The most successful schools are tenacious about making every minute of every day meaningful.

When I ask school leaders to explain their approach for extra time and help, I often get a "one item" answer, like, "We *offer* after school tutoring, but a lot of the students can't or won't stay." In order to make every minute count for academics, it is helpful to view opportunities for extra time like a menu. Restaurants provide breakfast, lunch, and dinner menus with a variety of food items. Mandate extra time, don't just offer it as a choice item. Build a menu of times before, during, and after school.

Before School

What time do you start school? What time do the academic classes actually begin compared to the time the very first student arrives on campus? I did a follow up visit last year at an ICU school that was really struggling. They were keeping a list of missing assignments but made little or no improvements to their *infrastructure*. I arrived on campus at 6:45 a.m. and sat at a picnic table with the first student to arrive on campus.

Mandate extra time, don't just offer it as a choice item.

The doors were still locked but he said this was the time he always arrived at school because his parents had to drop him off on their way to work. I asked him if he was on the ICU list and he told me he had five missing assignments. He said one of his teachers would let him inside the school at 7:00 a.m. "Will you work on your missing assignments when you get inside?" I asked. "Well, I really haven't thought about doing that but I guess I could," he answered. This school doesn't start their academic classes until 8:45 a.m. If they let him get started at 7:00 a.m., that converts one hundred five minutes per day and five hundred twenty-five minutes per week from wasted time to meaningful academic time. He said most of his five assignments would take him about twenty minutes meaning he would be totally caught up after just one day. Instead, he said he had owed these five assignments for more than a week and was not sure when or if he would complete them. In examining their morning routine further, I witnessed hundreds of students on campus (possibly the majority of the student body) by 7:45 a.m., socializing for an hour, and I only spoke with one student who was not on the list. I was so excited and could not wait to share with the ICU team that if they wanted to make every minute count before school, they had five hundred twenty-five minutes of down time that could be replaced with quality extra time.

As I spent the rest of the day with the teachers in small groups, all I heard was, "Our list is way too heavy," and, "We tell the students to come to our classrooms before school if they need help." Their paradigm was deeply seeded in helplessness and they totally ignored my recommendation to make every minute count. The purpose of sharing this is not to criticize the teachers and administration because I met some awesome people that day. My purpose is to emphasize that keeping a list of missing assignments, without the *infrastructure* improvements, will simply point out the extent of your student apathy which is not a solution. Thousands of assignments would be completed immediately if this school would change the way they do things **before school**.

During School

- One school's "lunch bunch" is a great example of providing extra time and help during the school day. Teachers and para-professionals are assigned "lunch bunch" as part of their daily schedule. All staff members make sure every student on the list goes to the ICU room instead of the cafeteria. According to the staff, it only takes students about ten minutes to eat lunch, leaving twenty minutes per day or one hundred minutes per week of quality extra time. This has become a part of the school culture and students view this as "extra time" and not punishment.

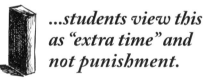 *...students view this as "extra time" and not punishment.*

- Lunch is certainly not the only time during the school day that can provide extra time/help. Some schools have alternate schedules for pep rallies, club time, and assemblies. These days provide an opportunity to add more minutes of extra academic time for students on the list. This is "extra time" provided during the school day and not punishment.

- At Watertown High School in South Dakota, students who owe assignments have to stay on student half-days once a month built into the schedule for teacher planning. Principal Mike Butts provides lunch at school for students on the ICU list while their friends go home or meet at a local fast food restaurant.

This is extremely effective because it converts approximately one hundred fifty extra minutes of meaningful time per month. Watertown does not just keep a list, they have changed their culture. Teachers get their planning time and the students have the extra time they need on these half days. According to Mike, "We cut our apathy in half after using the early release day for ICU."

Teachers in ICU schools say they take a vested interest in every assignment owed by the students they teach, even when the assignments are for another subject/teacher. When the teacher paradigm is, "Every minute counts for academics," they require students to complete missing assignments any time that "down time" occurs in their classroom.

...they require students to complete missing assignments any time that "down time" occurs in their classroom.

After School

"We just can't get them to stay!" Before you accept this excuse as a barrier to having an effective after school program, convert the parents. After a few months of staying after the parents, one of my veteran teachers said, "We truly underestimated our parents!" The apathetic parents want you to leave them alone, so don't. Initially, they will tell you they just can't get little Johnny a ride home. Using the bill collector's approach, keep calling and setting up meetings with parents until they get on board. Raise your expectations of your parents and consistently say, "Your child is behind and needs to stay after school to get caught up. We need you to find a relative or friend to provide transportation."

For some of the really stubborn parents, I (the principal) would call them and push a little harder for them to find transportation home. One of the hooks I used that really helped was, "If you can just find Johnny a ride home after school, then you will not have to worry about his academics. We will take care of it." For your slow, struggling students, establish set after school days (ex. Monday and Wednesday), which provides an individual long term plan for success. This is an extremely effective method that will keep your list small and students engaged during the school day. More importantly, you will establish a new paradigm among your students and their parents. Students know you will call, parents know it is worth it to find transportation, and teachers are no longer helpless.

The best after school programs:

1. Paid to stay. If grant money is available, then utilize it to pay teachers to stay after school, keeping in mind a large percentage of students struggle with math. If you can pay teachers, then be sure teachers strong in math (not necessarily the math teachers) are used whenever possible. Math teachers Mike Presley and Audrey Harrington held our after school ICU for 75 minutes in their classrooms (right next to each other) Monday through Thursday throughout the school year. English, science, reading, and social studies teachers would periodically stop by before they left for the day to help any of their own students. However, Mike and Audrey were getting paid to stay. When the state money ran out, I was able to get our PTO and local businesses to donate money to keep after school ICU going. I have visited many schools where teachers volunteer to stay after school, and this works for them, but paying teachers should always be the goal.

2. Use the same room(s) every day. I cannot tell you how important it was to our entire staff to know that "after school" was being held in Mike and Audrey's rooms every afternoon. Advisory teachers, administrators, guidance counselors, and all staff members could always tell students and parents the room number. Before we did

this it was always a hassle trying to figure out which teachers were helping after school and in what classroom to tell students to report. Students might stay after but end up wandering around the building or hiding in the bathroom because they, "Couldn't find the teacher's room." Consistency is key.

3. Develop a reliable parent contact system to get the parents on board. The **Power of ICU** team now has a solution that automatically emails and text messages parents within seconds of placing a missing assignment on the list. The purpose of developing this product was a result of the numerous requests for an easy-to-use list that would help with parent communication. Although personal phone calls to parents will always be necessary for engaging some students, the auto generated email and text message empowers teachers and drastically reduces the number of phone calls needed. It also empowers parents, because their child can no longer lie to them about being caught up on their school work. Parents are notified within seconds of an assignment not being completed. Teacher James Colbath was one of the first teachers to use it. He said, "The new auto-generated notification function with the ICU list is great. I typed in a missing assignment today and within 30 seconds I received this response, 'Please tell my son to contact me before the end of school today because I expect him to stay after school to complete his assignment. Thanks for letting me know.' This is a great tool!"

Continue to expand your extra-time menu. "Lunch Bunch" is better than nothing but is only one item - which is not enough. A full menu of extra time opportunities will allow you to customize a learning plan to meet the needs of every student. In a Brick House, down time turns into ICU time and every minute counts.

Chapter Sixteen

THEIR TIME

"ICU has caused some of our students to become lazy in class. They tell us they will just do the work later. Are we supposed to let them turn assignments in whenever they want?"

As with every new barrier you face, always keep in mind that letting students off the hook can never be an option. "They tell us," and, "Are we supposed to let them," makes it sound like the students make decisions and teachers are helpless. We had the same problem at Southside so we analyzed, discussed, and solved it. At first we thought the problem was ICU, but soon realized that keeping a list and holding students accountable could not "cause" laziness so it had to be our approach. Our discussion led us to ask ourselves a better question:

"How can we change the way we do things to hold students accountable and instill in them a sense of urgency for completing assignments?"

The challenge of finding an answer to this question unified our staff and we eventually found a solution - **THEIR TIME**. Extra time and extra help should be on **THEIR TIME** as much as possible. If students have to complete missing assignments when they would rather be somewhere else, they will realize a sense of urgency and complete assignments on time. This is not a prediction of what might happen when you effectively use their time, it is what will happen. You will stop hearing, "I will just do it later," when later is mandated on their time.

Do Not Let Extra Time Become Enabling

When I first changed my schedule at Southside, I built in too much extra time during the school day that took away from academic time. Additionally, some of our teachers built in one day a week during their class time for students on the list to get caught up. We found that if just one teacher routinely had a "catch up" day built into their weekly schedule, students would get lazy in other classes. "In my class I will let everyone who owes anything on ICU get caught up on Fridays," is extra time that is enabling because it lessens the urgency to work hard during class time. We were so determined to defeat apathy, that we created a new type of "lazy" problem.

Developing an extra time menu and being tenacious about using every minute of every day, as discussed in chapter fifteen, is critical. As you build your menu, realize the potential to also instill a sense of urgency by using their time as much as possible.

Before School Is Their Time

I visited a successful ICU school several months ago that was wasting twenty to thirty minutes before school. Students were very well behaved but socializing in the halls while the large ICU room was empty. They made an adjustment and started herding students on the list into the room and out of the hall. Within two weeks, teachers saw significant improvement in students completing work "on time" **because they did not want to miss THEIR TIME before school hanging out with their friends.**

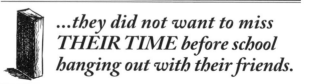

...they did not want to miss THEIR TIME before school hanging out with their friends.

Lunch

Most secondary students love lunch and hate to miss this time with their friends. Wilson ISD in Texas has extra time/help during lunch.

One teacher recently told me, "All last year getting Alisa to complete her assignments was like pulling teeth. This year she does all of her assignments on time because she absolutely hates to miss having lunch with her friends." Extra time/help during lunch is not a cure-all, but some students see this as their favorite time so they become engaged in class.

After School

When the bell rings to end the school day, **most students love to get home.** If they are on the ICU list, they need to stay after school on their time and complete anything on their lists. Originally, we tried to hold after school ICU just two days a week but found it was not enough. Once we made after school ICU every Monday-Thursday, we witnessed a significant improvement in our students' sense of urgency in completing assignments on time. One Texas junior high has after school ICU during the week plus "Friday Night Lights" every Friday afternoon which lasts longer. Mary Weiss, the principal at Hot Springs High School says, "All staff members make sure nobody sneaks out if they are supposed to stay for after school ICU. I occasionally will radio a bus driver to turn around and come back if we find that a student is on the bus but belongs in ICU." She and her excellent staff are tenacious. Students at these schools feel a sense of urgency in completing assignments and teachers never ask, "Are we supposed to let them turn assignments in whenever they want to?"

Alternate Schedule Days

Many students love alternate schedule days for pep rallies, club meetings, talent shows, faculty/student ballgames, and assemblies. Within your school, make ICU routine during these times and students will be internally motivated to stay off the list. At Hollister High School they have one school-wide assembly per month set up by the student council. Because students on the ICU list need "extra time" to clean up their list, they work on missing assignments during the assembly. Assistant Superintendent Chris Ford says, "**Students really like these assemblies** and so they work hard to stay off the list and we make sure they know that ICU is not punishment." In making changes in your school, never forget that it takes time for teachers and students to adjust. Trying something for one week or one month is not nearly long enough to establish a paradigm shift in your students. It is important to institute a new routine so they will understand this is the "way we do things now."

Dances

Some schools hold dances during the school day on special occasions like Valentine's Day. In a Brick House, all teachers and students know that special occasions become extra time for anyone on the ICU list. Always encourage students to stay caught up and ask for help so they will be able to attend. It is extremely important for students to know that needing extra time is not punishment. Additionally, it is confusing to students when missing the dance is also tied to behavior. For example, "Students who are on the ICU list and any student who has been in trouble recently will not be allowed to attend the dance," is not a good idea. Keep it simple, "Students who are on the ICU list will report to the ICU room during the dance to get caught up." Discipline issues must be kept separate.

ICU Days

An "ICU day" is usually a sixty to ninety minute time period when students who are on the list have extra time to get caught up. One school in Alabama set up an ICU day without telling their students ahead of time. During first period, the principal announced certain classrooms per grade level for students on the ICU list to report for extra time. I love the way he worded the announcement, "Some of you have fallen behind and need some extra time to get caught up. We are going to give you the extra time you need, right now." After the students on the list were settled in and working, the principal announced, "All students who do not need extra time, report to the gym." They had a sock hop (dance) in the gym. After ninety minutes and hundreds of assignments completed, all students were released and the academic schedule was followed for the rest of the day.

The students at Jackson Junior High School never tell their teachers they will, "Just do it later." Of the seven hundred fifty students, most have a sense of urgency and complete their assignments on time. Jackson has what they call a "Blitz Day" once a month from 12:40-1:50 p.m. Students on the ICU list meet with the their teachers while the other students attend a movie, play board games, play dodge ball or volleyball, etc. with concessions provided. Principal Cory Crosnoe and his creative staff adjust the lunch schedule and shorten seventh and eighth period so that missing class time is minimal. Keep in mind, if all they did for extra time was a regularly scheduled Blitz Day, it would cause laziness. Assistant Principal Mike Ford says, "Our regularly scheduled Blitz Day is so successful because our daily routine of before school, lunch detention, and after school extra time opportunities are so effective. Less than one percent of our students were on the ICU list for our last Blitz Day." Hold students accountable for completing assignments and do not let them tell you, "I will just do it later." When *later* is during **Their Time** your culture will instill a sense of urgency to stay off the list.

When "later" is during Their Time your culture will instill a sense of urgency to stay off the list.

Now the "good" students are taking advantage of the re-test option, not studying, and not taking the first round seriously.

How do you prevent re-tests from becoming a game? This can be a difficult issue to manage. Learning the standards is your primary purpose, therefore the solution cannot be to abandon retakes. According to Dr. Thomas Guskey, "To become an integral part of the instructional process, assessments cannot be a one-shot, 'do-or-die' experience for students. Instead, assessments must be a part of an ongoing effort to help students learn." It is critical to teach students that re-studying material not learned is important since most of the tests that adults take in the real world like driver's license, CPA, Bar exam, ACT, teacher licensing, etc. allow re-study and re-take.

How do you make re-taking tests a healthy part of your school culture and keep students from turning it into a game? Motivate students to study hard the first time by providing re-takes during **their time**, before or after school, during lunch, or during an assembly. As mentioned previously, students will have a sense of urgency when "later" is on their time. If teachers routinely give re-takes during class time, students will get lazy.

If teachers routinely give re-takes during class time, students will get lazy.

Another solution that will help avoid students turning retakes into a game is to require proof to the teacher that they have learned the material. Ann Smith, a ninth grade math teacher, told her students, "You can re-take this test if you complete these practice problems on the standard you are struggling with and then come in to grade it yourself. I will check over it and see if you are ready to re-take. If you need extra help, I can arrange a time for that. But you cannot re-take until you PROVE to me that you have learned the material you struggle with." Three to five problems can be enough to show proof of learning. Ann says, "The students grade the work themselves when they come to class and they show me they are ready. If they have put forth that much effort, then they can re-take. And re-take again. And re-take again. Each time with more work in between. This 'fix,' as you can imagine, cut my number of re-takes by quite a bit."

Jamie Hubbell, a middle school science teacher says, "At first, I was overwhelmed with the amount of students who wanted to re-take. Many of them came in just as unprepared the second time around as the first. I was frustrated with having to take on more work for myself even though the student weren't stepping up to the plate. So I started requiring my students to complete a task to prove they did, in fact, re-study the material. They could make color coded note cards, complete chapter questions, practice in the dreaded workbooks that came along with our textbooks, or other project activities on those skills. After implementing this practice, my top students would work hard on the front end like they always have. Everyone learned that if they did not work hard on the front end they would have to work hard on the back end. Either way, they would do the work and learn the skill."

One of my favorite re-study/re-take stories happened to Bob Brown, a high school geometry teacher in North Carolina. I was waiting in the principal's office and preparing for an afternoon presentation when the teacher walked in. "I read your book, Power of ICU, and it opened my eyes to a better approach. I decided to stop letting my students off the hook. One of my students had been totally shut down for several weeks. When I returned the test papers he received an F and his attitude reflected apathy. After class, I had a meeting with him and said the F was unacceptable. He seemed shocked. I told him I would come get him during lunch and we would go back over the material he did not learn. For two days we re-studied together but his attitude was still apathetic and he failed on his second try as well. I know he expected me to **leave him alone** but I stayed after him and we met two more times to go over the material. I think he intentionally blew the third re-take just to show me he was still in control and did not have to try. When I told him we were not finished he said, 'You are really serious about this aren't you?' I told him I would do whatever it took for him to learn and be successful. After repeating our re-study session, he scored 95% and was really excited. He had learned the material and he never looked back. Danny, I cannot tell you how excited I am about this student.

For the past two months, he has been one of my top students and tutors some of my other students with the same tenacity I showed with him. Thanks for the book (<u>Power of ICU</u>), I will never again allow learning to be optional with any of my students."

If your response to this success story starts, "but what about...?" then you missed the point. Stop with the helplessness. Staff members who reflect helplessness are not allowed in a Brick House. The actively disengaged teachers will try to seize every new problem and steer the group back into the cave by saying,

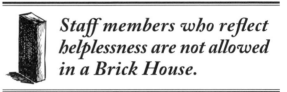

Staff members who reflect helplessness are not allowed in a Brick House.

"This ICU thing just isn't working, and things are actually getting worse." View every new problem as an opportunity for your staff to analyze, discuss, and solve together. Figure it out, find solutions, but stay after every child to learn the academic standards. Bob Brown never once asked, "But what about his grade?" He just tenaciously went after his apathetic student until he learned the material.

When extra time and retaking tests is on THEIR TIME, students will learn a sense of urgency. Re-taking tests will not turn into a game and, "I'll just do it later," will be a thing of the past.

Chapter Seventeen

Extra Time Merges With Extra Help

"Almost all students can master any content, given enough time and support."

– Benjamin Bloom, Mastery Learning Pioneer

Can you tell the difference between a student who is lazy and one that does not understand a concept? If you think you are always wise enough to know for sure, I think you are wrong. Never assume that a child is just lazy. Always assume the need for extra help and many of your students will surprise you and become engaged in the learning process. Only after extra help will you be able to discern laziness from lack of understanding.

Are You Rationing Extra Help?

According to the dictionary, rationing is the controlled distribution of resources or services. Rationing controls the size of one's allotted portion of the resource on a particular day or at a particular time. Are you unintentionally rationing extra help to your students? If there is a limited offering of extra help opportunities, then you will not meet the needs of every student. Some of the antonyms for the word "rationing" are smothering, heaping, showering, bombarding, and covering. As you hold students accountable for learning the academic standards, be sure your supply of extra help is unlimited. Do your students feel like they are being bombarded in extra help or rationed?

Make Extra Help Mandatory

Your extra time menu will naturally open up many opportunities to provide extra help for students. For the first two years of ICU at Southside, we provided substantial extra time opportunities and saw a drastic improvement in student engagement in every subject except math. Math assignments made up over ninety percent of our ICU list. We all thought the students just didn't like the subject (which is true for many) and just would not try. By Christmas time each year, about a third of our middle school math students were shutting down. This changed after we merged our menu of extra time before, during, and after school, into mandatory extra help. "I will be in my classroom thirty minutes before school every Tuesday morning to provide extra help for you," is a nice effort on the teacher's part but it misses the mark because it makes extra help optional. "If you need extra help, it is your responsibility to come in early on Tuesdays," limits extra help to one teacher and one time period which is not a menu of extra time/help. Instead, soak your students in extra help and weave it into the culture by making it mandatory and a readily available.

The expanded lunch concept has been implemented in many high schools. The philosophy is sound. "Students will be able to get extra help during lunch. Teachers will be *available* in their rooms on certain days for students to come in and *ask* for help." However, the success of this attempt at providing extra help for students is totally dependent on the implementation and approach. Smith High School takes the approach that this is an "opportunity for students to *ask* for help" and the hour lunch has had minimal effect of student success. Students have the "option" of socializing with friends for an hour or choosing to get the extra help they need. I know what I would chose. After four years of having the hour lunch for extra help, this high school is going to abandon it next year and the teachers are saying, "The hour lunch just did not work for us." On the other hand, at South Gibson High School in West Tennessee, ICU lunch is mandatory. Every day, during the last five minutes of third period, every teacher checks the list and the students are directed to ICU. All students on the list are required to meet with their teacher and the established *infrastructure* makes sure they attend.

Is it wise to provide extra time for extra help and then allow students the option of coming? Absolutely not! This is your turf. Control the way you do things and make extra help mandatory.

Extra Time + Assistance = Extra Help

Do not just babysit/watch while students complete assignments. What good is it to "monitor" students working on assignments if the monitor isn't actively seeking to help students understand concepts? One of the complaints I heard from parents over the years was, "I can't do the math. My daughter needs help with math and

> *Control the way you do things and make extra help mandatory.*

it is too hard for me." In a follow-up to an ICU high school, I visited a classroom full of students working individually at computers to recover a lost credit. The class was "monitored" by a coach reading the newspaper. He was a super guy but his paradigm towards his responsibility was to "monitor" rather than help. When I asked him if he was strong in math, he said no. He was babysitting extra time.

Provide assistance and engage/soak/immerse students with extra help. As previously mentioned, the first change we made at Southside was to put Mike and Audrey in charge of our after school program. This had a tremendous impact on student success because it merged extra time with extra help. Although a few students were simply lazy, the majority of the children who appeared to be apathetic were actually confused. Our teachers gained momentum when our students started asking if they could stay after school because they needed help! Students and teachers sharing the learning process became an integral part of our school.

Use Carefully Selected Students To
Increase Your Extra Help Work Force

Revisit the extra time ideas discussed earlier and carefully select students to provide the man power. Before school, for example, find students who would rather help other students learn than socialize. During a pep rally, use the peer tutors to increase your work force and turn this extra time into extra help. Train and monitor your peer tutors making sure they emphasize "learning the standard" over getting something turned in. Many students would rather get extra help from the student work force than their teachers.

 Many students would rather get extra help from the student work force than their teachers.

Students learn extremely well from their peers and they begin to pull for each other to complete assignments, learn the standards, and be successful on summative assessments. At some high schools, elective courses are offered in which students can earn credit through peer tutoring. If your school is near a university, use college education students who need observation and tutoring hours. Constantly brainstorm ways to increase your extra help work force so your resource supply meets the needs of all students.

Technology Explosion

Jonathan Bergmann and Aaron Sams, authors of the successful book Flip Your Classroom, Reach Every Student Every Day say, "No longer is the teacher physically needed to re-teach most topics. The technology explosion has made many of the difficulties of mastery learning easier to overcome." Bergmann and Sams developed the Flipped Classroom model in which students watch recorded lectures outside of class and complete their assignments, labs, and tests in class with their teacher available. Their video-tapes provide a library of extra practice lessons for students to watch as many times as needed.

Teachers should be provided a library of extra practice resources that are readily available and user friendly. However, until that happens, start developing your own. Just like a librarian continues to grow the number of books in their library, start accumulating your own extra practice resources (not more work sheets) and then add to it each year. During the school year, your teachers might provide at least one audio recorded lesson for every math standard. The goal will be to grow the number of samples per objective each year. Using a Smart Pen with microphones built into the tip, teachers can write out the lesson while recording their voice and students can watch these as many times (extra practice) as necessary at home or at school.

Technology allows teachers to follow their pacing guides during class time while students who fall behind get extra help with weaknesses during down time. The improvements in "standards-based" software programs allow teachers to provide targeted extra help for students who may learn better on the computer. Even if a student does not owe an assignment, down time should be used as extra practice to target specific student weaknesses so they can **move up** to the next learning level. A plethora of apps are now available for cell phones on targeted standards such as fractions, geometry, multiplication, order of operations, etc. that provide opportunities to soak students in extra practice.

In a Brick House, extra help is mandatory, the extra help work force is expanded, the use of technology is maximized, and the extra time menu merges into extra help opportunities.

Chapter Eighteen

CRUCIAL METAMORPHOSIS

"When you assign busy work as homework you bring shame to the entire teaching profession."

– Rick Wormeli

Students can complete every assignment and still not learn the academic standards. As painful as this is to admit, we need to comb through and cut out all insignificant assignments. Teachers' plates are already too full so consider this good news as it gives you a solid reason to take some things off your plate. Make sure every assignment is directly tied to the academic standards. What good is completed busy work? How many of your assignments miss the targeted academic standard? Teachers and students are too busy for busy work. Once again, this is an internal challenge totally within your control. Your school is overcrowded? What does that have to do with the quality of your assignments? You always get the worst kids in your classes? What does that have to do with the quality of your assignments? You do not like the principal, you are underpaid, and you are the only one who does hall duty? What does that have to do with the quality of the assignments you give to your students? Absolutely nothing!

Metamorphosis is defined as a marked change in appearance or function. The function of all assignments must transition from "something to do and complete" to "practice for learning." Student apathy has teachers chasing the shadow of, "Do your work."

ICU will dramatically reduce the number of missing assignments and you will clearly see that, "Do your work," is not enough. As one principal reported after one semester of ICU, "I could fill a dump truck with completed assignments that would not have been completed in the past." If the character of those completed assignment missed the targeted standard, what good did it do to hold his students accountable for completion?

I refer to the ICU list as a catalyst because it not only fuels students completing their work, it also stimulates teachers to improve the function of their assignments. One of our middle school Social Studies teachers at Southside,

...it also stimulates teachers to improve the function of their assignments.

Leslie Thompson, says "When we started putting our assignments on a list, it made me re-evaluate every single assignment. I realized that some of my assignments were just to get a grade in the grade book and had very little to do with learning the standards. Putting missing assignments on the list was time consuming so all of us were motivated to cut out busy work."

When the character of an assignment changes, a natural transformation takes place and assignments begin to appear as practice to students. The ICU list also fuels the metamorphosis because it places all assignments in plain view for every staff member to see. Even though this makes some teachers uncomfortable at first, it will motivate teachers to re-evaluate the value of each assignment. Teachers repeatedly say that the ICU list makes them accountable to other staff members. Leslie says, "The list makes you step back and examine every assignment because your fellow teachers know busy work when they see it." Quality assignments hit the targeted standard.

Dr. Rick Stiggins is the executive director of the ETS Assessment Training Institute in Portland, Oregon and one of the most respected educational consultants in the United States. Dr.

Stiggins says, "Students can hit any target that they know about and that holds still for them." The ICU list provides a target that they know about and holds still for them which is one of the reasons it re-ignites student engagement. *The crucial metamorphosis, however, is when your ICU list of missing assignments changes to your ICU list of missing practice. The target must change.* The new target is the list of academic standards.

Fuel The Metamorphosis

If teachers change to a **standards based grade book,** then it will give momentum to the necessary transition. This type of grade book specifically catalogues weaknesses, strengths, and levels of learning. Each box in your grade book becomes a known and stationary target for the students.

Just as the ICU list itemizes missing *assignments* for each student, a **mastery learning chart** itemizes each student's proficiency for the various *standards.* The picture on the next page shows a master learning chart that Audrey Harrington uses for her middle school math students. The students choose a nickname to reduce competition and avoid embarrassment. The nicknames are listed down the left side of the chart and the standards (SPI - Student Performance Indicators) are listed across the top. Students had to show Audrey they learned the standard at a certain level in order to earn a star in the box. She says the mastery learning chart was extremely helpful, because it was in plain view for her and her students to see every day. "Each standard is now something they see and can work toward. The chart makes learning measurable and attainable. Students are challenged to improve their level of learning." The mastery learning chart serves as a

The mastery learning chart serves as a "snapshot" to target weaknesses per class period.

"snapshot" to target weaknesses per class period. For example, if a significant number of students in first period did not have stars for order of operations, then she would spend a few minutes re-teaching this first period even though the other class periods had weaknesses in other areas.

Anne Davies, a highly respected education author, consultant and researcher, teaches that involving students in the classroom assessment process is critical for student engagement. She says, *"When teachers emphasize learning and performance, rather than competition and grades, students are more likely to be intrinsically motivated."*

All of my students were thrilled each time they earned a star. The biggest celebration came when a student earned seven or eight stars at once after falling behind and then finally "getting it."

- Audrey Harrington
8th Grade Math

Are the students coming to your classroom daily to, "Do their work," and hope they learn the standards? Or do you marinate your students in "practice for learning" the academic standards? Drop the terms *work* and *homework* and replace them with *practice* and *extra practice*. Your language is critical! It will change the appearance of assignments for your students. Parents relate positively to *practice* and *extra practice* as well. Baseball practice, football practice, soccer practice, choir practice, and band practice are already ingrained in their minds. You need *extra practice* in dribbling or *extra practice* on this song is common language in their daily lives. If your assignments are practice for learning, be sure your language reflects that.

Your school culture reflects a house of sticks/straw if any of your teachers continue to tell students, "Do all of your assignments, turn them in on time, and you will have no problems passing my class." This says to the student, the main purpose of the assignments is *effort* and *passing* which weakens your culture because the main target of learning the standards is left to chance.

How do your assignments appear to your students? What is the character of every assignment at your school? Is your paradigm toward assignments, "Students must DO THE WORK because it is their job?" Or, "Every assignment is PRACTICE to help them learn the standards?" This metamorphosis is critical.

In A Brick House:

- Students hear all staff members refer to assignments as "*practice*."
- When a student has an academic weakness, they consistently hear, "*extra practice*."
- Teachers routinely use the list of standards with **Academic CPR** to engage and internally motivate (snowball effect) students who fall behind.
- Everyone consistently refers to the ICU list of **missing assignments** as the ICU list of **missing practice**.

Chapter Nineteen

HALLS OF HARMONY

I never heard a cuss word until I was in junior high. A guy sitting next to me on the bus one day said, "Damn," really loud and I asked him what that meant. He was floored! For the remaining twenty minute bus ride home, he enthusiastically presented me with my first Professional Development Course (unpaid) on cussing. His effective in-service covered the main cuss words with strict orders to not discuss these words with my parents. Of course, since I had never heard my parents use any of these words I thought they did not know them. They showed wisdom in speaking a healthy language every day in our home. It was their home, they were the parents, and they chose the language spoken there. My mom was a pretty good singer, dad was below average, and you would never want to hear them sing a duet. However, the harmony in their language was consistent with all three of their boys. The language in our home was so positive and full of hope that we had no choice but to succeed. Everyone in the Hill's Brick House pulled for each other every day.

Harmony or Discord? What do your students hear when they enter your school? Too many of our students are raised in discord, disagreement, and chaos at home. I had one seventh grade boy who lived in silence because his father never spoke to him. In many homes, discouragement is the language everyone speaks. The house is a war zone where nicknames like stupid, idiot, dummy, and worthless are stamped on the children daily. Their lives have been violated and life is staring them down. Your school culture must be a shelter, shield, and strong tower of encouragement, support, hope, and harmony.

Harmony in Everyday Language

If/Then Threats

If you don't do your work, then you will not pass.
If you don't do your work, then you will never be successful.
If you turn your work in late, then you will lose ten points per day.
If you don't study, then you will get an F.
If you don't start trying harder, then your grades will suffer.

In my early years in education, I used these if/then threats repeatedly because I did not think there was any other option. Every other teacher used if/then threats so I assumed that they worked.

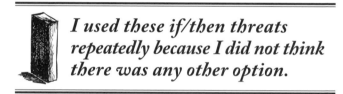

I used these if/then threats repeatedly because I did not think there was any other option.

However, when we started keeping a list and providing mandatory extra time and help for our students, the if/then threats started sounding out of place. As I started studying my apathetic students and dysfunctional families, I realized that if/then threats can trigger defiance and distrust in many of the students you are trying to teach. I believe it is because too many of our students live in an if/then home and come to school each day hearing the Big Bad Wolf whispering:

If mom doesn't get a job, then we won't be able to pay the rent.
If mom doesn't pay the rent, then we will have to move again.
If dad gets drunk tonight, then he might slug mom again.
If dad gets mad at me, then he might leave us again.
If granny dies, then I will have no place to live.

These are very real and dangerous threats that sometimes suck the life out of our students. Many of you reading this book were smothered with similar if/then threats growing up and can testify that the threat of not passing or losing ten points is meaningless when living with dangerous threats at home.

It is counterproductive to turn the ICU list into a new if/then threat. Statements like, "If you would just do your work, then you would be able to go to the pep rally," or, "If you would just do your work on time, then you would get to eat lunch with your friends," are counterproductive and unnecessary.

Replace threats with positive statements like, "I want you to eat lunch with your friends, but you need the extra time to stay caught up. Do you need any help in completing this assignment?" Needing extra time or help is okay and the students must hear that from every adult. Missing a pep rally because they need extra time cannot sound like punishment to the student or they will become defiant. "I hate for you to miss the pep rally today but you really need the extra time and possibly extra help. What can we do to avoid missing the next one?" This is not a small thing. Stop the if/then threats!

One Texas ICU school recently had a team visit from a nearby school. They wanted to see ICU in action. Confident that his teachers and students were on the same page, Principal Darin Jolly allowed the visitors to stop any teacher or student and ask them questions about ICU. One visitor asked a seventh grader, "Are you in trouble for being on the ICU list?" The student replied, "Yes, at home. Not at school. ICU helps me at school." This school won the war on student apathy last year and every student completes every assignment routinely. And, the response of the student reflected that teachers there never use threats to get students to complete assignments.

"I'm giving you exactly what you deserve."

Words can kill or give hope to your students. When teachers say,

"I'm giving you exactly what you deserve," it can kill a child's spirit. Teachers allow students to sit and do nothing in their class while rationalizing that, "It is their choice," if the assignments get done. While presenting **Power of ICU** to a large high school staff in Texas, one of the assistant principals was emotional in his desire to change some of the harmful language he hears consistently from some of his teachers. He said, "I absolutely hate to hear a teacher tell a student they are giving them exactly what they deserve (meaning some type of failing grade) because it just takes the life out of the student." How can we say we are giving them what they deserve when they deserve a positive learning culture and a unified school staff that tenaciously supports them? In a Brick House, this phrase is unacceptable.

"I've tried everything."

This is another toxic statement frustrated teachers say to students. This declaration cuts, maims, and it kills! My amazing dad, Marvin Hill, died from prostate cancer many years ago. After a variety of treatments extended dad's life, his doctor finally said the words we had all dreaded, "I've tried everything." I will never forget the heavy burden of hopelessness in those words. Our hearts were shattered.

At Southside, our counselor, Linda Crutcher, would scold any parent who said, "I've tried everything," in front of their child. Linda generously soaked every student, teacher, and parent in HOPE everyday making her office the safest room in the school. She always had a new plan telling students, "And if this does not work, I have another idea, but I think this will work." Reckless words pierce like a sword. Words of hope hold students accountable because they will not want to disappoint you.

"Today is a Fresh start."

Students should hear this phrase from every adult, every day in your school. Each day is a fresh start and hopeless students are starving to hear these words. Teachers say they care about their students but what good does it do if the students do not know it? You can do much with words like these: "Will, you know you drove me crazy yesterday and I was really upset with you, but today is a fresh start. We are going to have a great day."

Ohio's Southeast Middle School librarian, Pam Cottrell, was really excited about the immediate culture shift she witnessed as a result of ICU. On my follow up visit she said, "The best thing about ICU right now is that we get to know the students on a more personal level. They hear that we, the entire staff, are here to *help* them not to *get them*."

> *"The best thing about ICU right now is that we get to know the students on a more personal level."*

The language you choose as a staff is powerful and it has nothing to do with money for resources, the newness of your building, the poverty rate, the number of transient students, the leadership in your district, or parent support. Your daily language has the power to kill or give life.

Harmony in Academic Language

"Are you going to grade this?"

Even the top students consistently ask this question and it drives us crazy. Why do they keep asking it? Control! The students have us on autopilot and this is the clearest evidence that they want to maintain control. They ask because they are trying to determine: a) "Am I going to do this assignment?" and b) "If I decide to do it, how much effort will I give?" Students, especially the ones who care, will continue to control you with, "Are you going to grade this?" as long as you keep *reacting* to it. Zig Ziglar says that we either **react** or **respond** to questions. To **react** is a bad thing just like having a reaction to medicine. When I taught eighth grade science

I would frequently react with, "I have told you to stop asking me that question so now I am going to DOUBLE THE GRADE." I now realize my reaction was counterproductive. Ziglar points out that when we **respond** to medicine it is a good thing. As a part of your Brick House, teachers should respond to the question, "Are you going to grade this?" in harmony.

Try this response:

"I want to see what you have learned."

With this simple response you harmoniously emphasize two important points using consistent academic language:

1. You are in control and will make decisions about what is graded and what is not graded - every assignment is significant and maximum effort is expected.
2. You redirect students to the main purpose, learning.

Remember, getting every student to complete every assignment is just the beginning. The main purpose is for students to learn the standards and for their grades to be a better reflection of learning. Keep building!

 The main purpose is for students to learn the standards and for their grades to be a better reflection of learning.

"I know you said the project is due on Friday, but what if I don't turn it in on Friday?"

Doesn't this one get under your skin too? It is obviously another control question. The student is trying to decide if he is going to do the project based upon your answer. In trying to wrestle control back, we generally blurt out (react), "If you don't turn it in until Monday, the best you can make is a B." Or, "I don't take late work." Or, "I automatically count off ten points per day for late work." Why do we keep spinning our wheels in the mud using these ridiculous threats? How can you predict the level of learning before you see the project?

I suggest this healthy response:

"I do not know what your grade will be because I haven't seen it yet." You might even add, *"Your grade will reflect what you have learned, so I need to see it before I grade it."* This puts you back in the driver's seat. When you react, you handcuff yourself. When you respond, you free yourself up to make a professional decision.

"At our school we don't *let* our students re-take tests, we *require* it."

"Letting" your students redo work or re-take tests is an enabling phrase. However, if every staff member consistently replaces the word "let" with the word "require" you establish higher expectations. Students must hear, "You will be required to redo sloppy work. You will be required to restudy material you have not learned. You will be required to retake tests you do not pass." Expect them to learn the material and require them to show you they learned it.

I will never forget the hopelessness in the eyes of one of my eighth grade boys when he said to me, "Mr. Hill, I really wish that I had never been born." He was not trying to manipulate me. He was serious. As I thought about my incredible staff of adults at Southside, I was thankful no one used phrases like, "I've tried everything with you." I was able to get him started on his missing assignments and was confident he would hear harmony in our halls. He would hear positive language full of hope every day and he had no choice but to succeed.

Is the language in your school so positive and full of hope that your students have no choice but to succeed? Make harmony in the halls a priority in the war against student apathy. We cannot repair the broken down walls of their homes so we must build the walls of their school home Brick House Strong!

Chapter Twenty

WHAT ABOUT THE TOUGHEST STUDENTS?

My oldest daughter Kellie works as a critical care nurse practitioner at Vanderbilt Hospital in Nashville. She says that the common procedure for every patient is to be given a *primary survey* upon entering the ICU. The *primary survey* includes assessing blood pressure, temperature, and all the vital signs. Often, a diagnosis and treatment can be started based on the *primary survey*. However, with some patients a *secondary survey* is necessary to gather more specific information. The patient is thoroughly checked from head to toe in order to properly diagnose and treat him. An EKG, ultrasound, MRI, or X-Ray are examples of *secondary survey* methods that provide information necessary for targeted treatment and improved health.

Thankfully, doctors do not give up on patients who do not respond to the *primary survey*. They are tenacious about finding answers. Most of us went in to the teaching profession to make a difference. Do you still believe you can make a difference? "Some of these kids just can't be helped," is a common statement by teachers who have become calloused. This is a false assumption so don't allow this in your thinking. If you don't think you can make a difference, then you have lost your purpose. When we lose our purpose, we lose our passion! The most apathetic students are the ones who do not initially respond and for various reasons, they will continue to resist and tell us to just leave them alone. Instead of getting discouraged, view these students as a test of your tenacity.

Stay after them by continuing to gather information. In order to get your toughest students engaged, you will need more specific information, a secondary survey, to diagnose and treat them successfully.

Gather and Share Information

We had many transient students at Southside, so every staff member routinely gathered information and shared it with each other. Our experience with transient students taught us that the better we knew our students the better chance we had to engage them in school. We viewed every new student like a patient in the hospital ICU unit. Our *primary survey* started with our secretary the moment they stepped foot on campus and started filling out *We viewed every new student like a patient in the hospital ICU unit.* the registration form. The registrar then had a meeting with the parent or guardian continuing to gather *primary* information. Our guidance counselor followed up with calls to the former school(s) immediately and was persistent in finding someone who knew the student personally. Except for confidential information, all information was shared daily among the staff. The following is an example of how I gathered information, as an administrator, while handling discipline.

A few years ago in the middle of the school year, we had a new eighth grade boy (we will call him Kenny) who was in trouble for cursing at another student in PE class. The young man's body language was defiant and I could tell he did not trust me. (Notice my emphasis is on gathering information.)

Hill: Who do you live with?

Kenny: I live in foster care.

Hill: Are you being treated right? Do they take good care of you? Do you have a decent bed, food, and clothes? Are they nice to you?

Kenny: (I could tell he was already relaxing) Yes, they treat me pretty good, actually.

Hill: I am glad you are here at Southside. Is everybody here treating you right? Are my teachers working with you to get settled in?

Kenny: Yes, everything is going pretty good so far except I said "damn" just now and Coach Wheeler heard me.

Hill: Well, we can deal with that in a minute. Do you want to tell me how you got into foster care?

Kenny: Mom is in Georgia and can't take care of me. My dad was just sentenced to prison and I was staying with him. He is going to be gone a long time.

Hill: I am glad you are here and in a good foster home. Besides foster care, where would you like to live? Dad is not an option and I am sorry about that. Is mom a good option or is there another good possibility?

Kenny: Mom is not an option but I really hope I get to go live with my grandparents. They say they want me and are trying to get me. I really think living with them would be good.

Hill: If you ever need/want to contact them, let me know and I will see if it is something we can arrange for you during your school day. By the way, are you on the ICU list? Do you owe any assignments? (Remember there is power in the list.)

Kenny: Nope, I am all caught up on everything. I'm not on the list for anything.

Hill: Ok, I am going to have to send you to ISS tomorrow because we don't cuss at Southside (at least the students can't) but if you need anything – shirt, paper, pencil, anything, you come sit in that chair and wait on me.

Before he left my office we shook hands and I went over the proper way to shake hands and reminded him to, "Be sure to look me in the eye." During this routine discipline meeting, I was able to learn Kenny's story and establish rapport. Over the years I learned that Kenny and students like him would probably be in some type of trouble soon anyway so our approach became proactive rather than reactive. Just like the hospital *secondary survey* thoroughly checks the patient from head to toe, your school staff must regularly gather and share the stories of your toughest students. Never leave them alone!

Guidelines for Secondary Survey

1. Meet with the student individually and make the meeting informal and comfortable. Don't sit behind your desk.
2. Never discuss behavior or grades.
3. Listen and don't lecture.
4. Get the student engaged in conversation about herself.
5. If the student does not open up, then try again with a different adult. You never know which adult they will trust the most.
6. At some point, ask if they are on the ICU list. The list is a non-threatening catalyst so when you ask about it, they hear that you care. If they answer yes, ask them if they need anything and if there is anything you can do to help.

Suggested Questions for Secondary Survey

HOME:

1. Who do you live with?

    Stay away from questions like: "Do you live with your mom or dad?" Many of our "toughest students" are tired of explaining their living conditions. "Who do you live with" is open and easy for the student to explain as little or as much as they want. It is a great opening question.

2. Outside of school who do you look up to the most?

    What did he/she do in your life to become important to you?

3. If you could call one person, who would that be?

4. Who can make you laugh?

5. Do you have an uncle, aunt, grandparent, older sibling, cousin, pastor, Sunday School teacher, junior pro coach, police officer, or former step parent who you have a close relationship with?

SCHOOL:

1. Who is your favorite teacher or adult at our school?

   Try to get them to explain why.

   Ask them how often they see this teacher/adult during the school day.

2. Who is your favorite teacher of all time including every school you have attended?

   If they attended your feeder school and they mention one of those teachers, this could be important information.

3. Is there a student (besides your best friend) who you respect? Is there a student who doesn't judge you and they always treat you right even though they don't run with your group?

If you are thinking, "Apathetic students won't answer these questions," I disagree. In dealing with thousands of students and specifically focusing on the most apathetic students throughout my career, I never had a student refuse to answer these questions. My wife, Debbie, a high school graduation coach agrees. She says, "I don't think I've ever had a high school student (apathetic or not) that would not talk to me if I establish the right kind of rapport with them. If they think they are safe and not at risk of getting judged or in trouble, I find they actually like talking about themselves." Her role puts her in direct contact with students shutting down and thinking seriously about dropping out. She says listening and gathering information is critical in re-engaging her students.

It is very important when trying to reach the toughest students, to find the right person to ask the right questions to gather as much information as possible. New information about a student empowers you to develop a new plan of action.

Academic Progress Hearing, Code Blue Hearing, Family Day

After gathering as much information about the student as possible, hold a short meeting with all teachers, parents, and/or guardians to establish the new plan of action. Bob Devine, secondary supervisor in Pocatello, Idaho, uses the term *Academic Progress Hearings* and says he got the idea from the Discipline Hearings traditionally held for serious behavior problems. When teachers notice a student is shutting down and not showing up for extra time/help sessions, the school will call an academic hearing that parents/guardians must attend. Behavior and discipline are not the focus of the meeting, only academics are discussed. Bob says, "Our academic hearings have been extremely effective in re-engaging students in the learning process."

Principal Phil Rogers and his staff at South Gibson County High School call their intervention meetings *Code Blue* meetings because code blue in a hospital means "needs immediate attention." A *Code Blue* meeting is called anytime a student has too many missing assignments or if they stay on the ICU list too long. The list is used as a catalyst for knowing who needs immediate attention.

Mark McAllister, principal at P.R. Leyva Middle School in New Mexico, and his staff are having great success since implementing the following in addition to the automatic text message and email for each single missing assignment:

3-4 Missing Assignments: Direct contact with parent. This contact serves to notify the parent, ask for specific support, and determine if the phone number in the database is correct.

5-7 Missing Assignments: **Academic Hearing** - Face to face meeting with parent to discuss a new plan of action.

8-10 Missing Assignments: They call this *Family Day* because they require a parent to come to school and sit with their child until all missing assignments are complete.

Mark says, "This works great because after one *Family Day*, the parent makes sure their child does not get to that point again. They do not want to spend a half day at school and their child doesn't want them at school either."

Jackson Middle School implemented the *Family Day* in an attempt to engage their toughest students. Within a week they said, "It worked like gangbusters. Two of the students 'urgently' turned in all assignments before *Family Day* because they did not want their parents to come sit with them at school and all of our toughest students completed every assignment."

I have shared the *Family Day* concept with several ICU schools looking for answers. The feedback has been very positive. One teacher said she had never seen anything like it in her twenty one years of teaching. Never leave them alone and never leave their parents alone!

Fresh Start Plan of Action

No matter what you call your intervention hearing, *secondary survey* information is applied to a *Fresh Start* plan of action. In a hospital ICU, the more serious the condition, the more doctors and nurses are needed. Take the same approach with your toughest students.

> *In a hospital ICU, the more serious the condition, the more doctors and nurses are needed. Take the same approach with your toughest students.*

They need every significant person in their home life and at school on board with the new plan. For example, if you learned about a favorite teacher or relative, be sure they attend the meeting or are somehow involved. Constantly adjusting a student's academic intervention plan is no different than doctors who constantly update treatment plans for patients in serious or critical condition. A new plan of action serves as a fresh start, sends the message, "We will never leave you alone," and restores hope to the student and staff members.

Your toughest students need routines much more than other students. Knowing the patterns empowers you to be proactive. Make it a priority to get them back on track and into the routine ahead of time, instead of waiting for them to get too far behind. This is why the ICU list is a catalyst. It gives you a daily snapshot of who owes what. You should never be shocked when your toughest students try to revert back to apathy. Instead, build in steps to constantly get them back on track.

Chapter Twenty-One

ESPRIT DE CORPS

In June of 1990 I was assigned to be the principal at Southside K-8 school in Lebanon, Tennessee. Notice I said "assigned." Nobody wanted to be at Southside. They had eight different principals during a span of eleven years, with most staying only one year. I had applied for a K-5 school but was "assigned" to Southside.

In July, before I had even met the staff, my wife and I were looking at houses. At one particular house the realtor handed me the real estate report. While my wife was looking around, I noticed this statement in bold print at the end of the real estate report:

This house is zoned to Southside K-8; however, you will probably want to apply for an out of zone waiver to attend Byers-Dowdy Elementary.

When I asked the realtor about it, he explained that Southside had a bad reputation which could hurt the sale of the house. My blood was boiling and I was embarrassed! I had just been named the principal of this school and realtors were telling people, "You probably don't want your children at Southside, steer clear." "There is no way this will continue," I thought. "We are already underpaid and underappreciated; we will not be disrespected within our own community!"

On the first day with my staff, I introduced myself briefly and then asked two new teachers to stand next to me. I told the Southside staff about looking for a house and then pulled out the real estate report. I told them where the house was located and then read the report to them:

This house is zoned to Southside K-8; however, you will probably want to apply for an out of zone waiver to attend Byers-Dowdy Elementary.

Without waiting for a response, I said, "Although I know there are some great teachers in this room, you all have to own the fact that Southside's reputation stinks in our community. Except for me and these two new teachers, the rest of you have been a part of allowing Southside to become a bad school in the eyes of Wilson County. Let's watch this brief but powerful documentary and discuss how we can build an outstanding school."

I showed them *Learning in America*, an ABC news research project (1990) which investigated the common characteristics of exemplary schools and school systems across America. Its primary objective was to study the educational process at its best. More specifically, the study wanted to find schools and systems that work and campuses where students and teachers perform with skill, enthusiasm, and success.

All of the successful schools cited in the show were from average to below average income levels with average to above average minority populations. The investigative team said teachers, students, parents, and the business community openly praised their school. In visiting and studying each of the exemplary schools chosen, their conclusion was a simple but powerful commonality - the staff members at every school had established *esprit de corps* among all stakeholders.

Esprit de corps is the capacity of a group of people to pull together persistently and *...the staff members at every school had established esprit de corps among all stakeholders.*

consistently in pursuit of a common purpose. The morale of the staff members in each of the schools reflected unity in spirit and there was no doubt their common purpose was the children.

After watching the program, I asked my staff to analyze the morale in our school. The teachers were honest as they concluded,

"Our Southside staff does not believe in Southside. We are not proud of our school and many of us send our own children to other schools." I fell in love with my teachers that day because in almost everyone's voice I heard passion for children which would become our common ground. Looking back on it, they were all starving for a positive culture.

We discussed how the successful schools in the video showed a strong commitment to relationship building and respect between teachers, administration, and the community. We needed every adult to pull together and consistently put our students first. We decided as a team to establish Southside as a highly respected school within our own community. We wanted adults in the community saying, "You want your child to go to Southside, it is a great school." Was this a measurable and achievable goal? We found out that it was.

We had a lot of work to do internally to build a strong culture for our children. Our staff needed to believe in our school. Externally we needed to drastically improve our image in the community. Three years later, after lots of hard work, visitors and parents were beginning to comment on the team spirit they experienced at our school. Our teachers were bringing their own children with them to our school and I started receiving requests from teachers at other schools to transfer to Southside. Then, one of my teachers placed a real estate report on my desk. It was a full page advertisement from one of the largest realtors in Wilson County. In bold letters it said:

"YOU HAVE BEEN ASKING AND NOW WE HAVE THEM. HOUSES AVAILABLE IN THE SOUTHSIDE SCHOOL ZONE."

We did it! I called an emergency faculty meeting to celebrate.

Establishing *Esprit de Corps*

Children come first - no matter what! Esprit de corps has nothing to do with hanging out with each other, going shopping with each other, or even liking each other. It does require that all staff member put the children first in every decision. If everyone pulls in the same direction every day, your disagreements will always find common ground in what is best for your students.

Lay your "relationship swords" down before entering the building. The Civil War is over. Every staff member must lay their relationship swords down because you do not have the time or energy to verbally sword fight during the school day. Very simply, arguing and cutting each other down is not allowed!

Think about the unity that permeates throughout a school when tragedy strikes. A high school I am familiar with experienced the unexpected death of one of their teachers a few years ago. This school had a reputation for arguing among themselves and cutting each other down in the community. There was a noticeable unity among the staff, students, and parents as everyone gathered around the flag pole to hold hands and grieve. For a few days everyone left their relationship swords at the door. Sadly, within days, the adult staff was back at it, arguing and cutting each other down.

At your school, don't just try to "do better." Embrace the belief that, "when the adults in the building are verbally sword fighting, the children are the ones who suffer." Collegiality among teachers is required and no relationship swords are allowed.

***Esprit de corps* means that you have each other's backs every day.** Commit to proactively support each other every day. Recently, at the end of a presentation, I was approached by a teacher who shared this. "I like the way you say 'Declare War on Apathy' because teachers working together can save these children. I was a soldier who fought in Iraq and Afghanistan and soldiers at war always pull for each other unconditionally. We need that same unity at this school. I cannot believe the backbiting and senseless arguing that goes on among our staff. Keep saying 'Declare War.'"

If you are in a fox hole fighting for your lives, does it really matter if you LIKE each other? You are in a war together and you must have each other's backs or you will die. Listen to the *Esprit de corps* in America during WWII as Bob Grant, the King of NYC talk radio, reflects:

"Not only was America at its best on the battlefield, but here at home as well - scrap drives, rationing, the saving of cooking oils, the paper drives, the buying of war bonds and war stamps. The patriotism of Americans was a demonstration of our citizens at their finest! We never wavered; we never doubted; we never spoke ill of our leaders. We had a war to be fought and won. Any second-guessing or any criticism would have to wait until victory was ours. When the national anthem was played, we all stood at attention and silently prayed for a brother or father or son fighting in some land we had hardly heard of before. There were many people who did not like Franklin Delano Roosevelt, but the nation was more unified during those World War years than it had been since anyone could remember."

Build a "verbal wall" around your school. A verbal wall is a very powerful thing. During my four years as assistant principal at Lebanon High School, I noticed the parents and staff members at a nearby private school never criticized "Their School." Adults building a protective verbal wall around a private school is easy to understand. Why would you criticize "your school" when you are paying thousands of dollars to send *Build a "verbal wall" around your school.* your child there? For example, if a student at Lebanon High School had a major discipline offense, everybody in the community was talking about it and it would be on the front page of the local newspaper. On the other hand, when a student at the private school committed a major offense, the local newspaper never knew it happened. They had problems like everybody else; they just kept everything "in house."

Discuss your school's reputation in the community with your staff. You may find that the reason your school is disrespected within your own community is because you have been verbally criticizing yourselves in public. NO MORE! Simply start bragging about your school at every opportunity. "I love teaching at Southside." And, "We are having a great year at Southside, things are going great." At ballgames, the grocery store, church, and while socializing with friends, build a "verbal wall" around our school. You may experience community members trying to bait you into criticizing your school. Every teacher has heard the sarcasm when someone says, "Well, it's almost over (summer), I bet you are excited to get back to those kids?" To which you can respond, "Actually, I can't wait to get back to school. I love my job!"

Your paradigm will shift as you start viewing your school as a family. Co-workers will still get on each other's nerves, but you get over it because you are all in the same school family.

 Co-workers will still get on each other's nerves, but you get over it because you are all in the same school family.

Some of the parents will still be crazy, but they are your crazy parents, so stop criticizing them in public. And no matter what the students' stories, they are your students and you always protect your own.

Principals should take the lead in building a verbal wall around their teachers. Several years ago a photographer/reporter for the local newspaper offered this observation while waiting to take a picture, "Danny, in all my years of covering Southside, the one thing that always stands out to me is the way you brag on your teachers and staff members. You always use the word 'fantastic' when describing your people."

Create times during faculty meetings for staff members to share a compliment they have received at the ballpark, church, or while shopping. As the compliments grow they will motivate you to keep getting better. During a tough time period, hold a staff meeting to recharge your batteries. The entire meeting may include:

- Sharing positive stories and compliments from parents and community members that validated your team.

- Sharing student success stories that motivate and reinforce the positive difference you are making in children's lives.

- Your guidance counselors may share some of the students' heartbreaking stories to revive your *teacher hearts* and remind everyone how badly your students need you.

You do not need a grant to have *esprit de corps*. You do not need additional staff to have *esprit de corps*. *Esprit de corps* has nothing to do with how many economically disadvantaged students you serve or if your parents value education or not. *Esprit de corps* is not bound by your past reputation. It is your choice. If you expect 100% of your students to become engaged in school, then 100% of your staff members must be engaged. They must pull together persistently and consistently in pursuit of a common purpose. Children come first - no matter what!

Chapter Twenty-Two

SWEEPERS

It was January when I received the email from my two middle school physical education teachers, Dr. Fred Wheeler and Liz Starnes. Fred and Liz decided to challenge all of our adult staff to run or walk in the Music City Half Marathon in late April. Fred runs eight miles every morning before school and Liz's favorite workout is called INSANITY. Our middle school students always worked up a sweat because their teachers believed in and modeled physical fitness. I was surprised when I discovered that twenty one of our ninety one adults had accepted their challenge, paid their money, and started meeting after school to train. Fred and I bought everyone red and white shirts with Southside written on the front to wear while training. Our family spirit was once again on display as our community witnessed Southside staff members training together every weekend and most afternoons.

In the days immediately following the email challenge, I discussed with several people what motivated them to sign up to run. The answer was always the same, "Fred and Liz promised in the email they would be SWEEPERS and stay back with anyone who started to struggle. I just did not want to be embarrassed by being the last one to finish and alone. Fred and Liz promising they would be there with me if I needed them was what motivated me." I went back and re-read the email and the word SWEEPERS jumped out at me this time. My daughter Kellie had asked me to run with her, so I had not even thought about how it might feel to run and finish last and alone.

I asked Fred and Liz exactly what they meant by the word and they said, "You know, like a broom that keeps going back over an area to make sure that every piece of dirt is swept up. Not one person will be left behind. We will continue to drop back throughout the race and keep our eyes on anyone who falls behind. We will only get involved if they need our help but our goal is for all twenty-one of us to **finish the race, regardless of the time it takes.**"

"We will continue to drop back throughout the race and keep our eyes on anyone who falls behind."

Throughout January and February our half marathon team encouraged each other daily. A half marathon is 13.1 miles and most of us had never run that far. Anytime a team member improved by even a half mile, we all celebrated with verbal praise and emails. By mid-March, our entire team was in great shape. However, Randi, our seventh grade reading teacher, missed a couple days of school and was extremely distraught when she learned that she had bronchitis. On the day she returned to school, she told Fred and Liz that she did not think she would have time to recover and get back in shape. I was in agreement with Randi but my opinion did not matter as they continued to encourage her and talked her into remaining on the team. They kept saying, "Twenty-one start and twenty-one finish!"

The day before the race, Fred and I surprised the team with new shirts that said, "Southside Half Maniacs" on the front and "No Teacher Left Behind" on the back. We thought this would help us find each other during the race but we were wrong. After riding to the race together in a school bus, we arrived in Nashville to discover over thirty thousand people. My daughter and I found it difficult to stay together because the streets were so crowded and I never spotted any of our team members throughout the half marathon. However, having her with me was an encouragement to keep going and she held me accountable to keep moving toward the goal. I did not set any speed records that day, but crossing that finish line was one of the most rewarding experiences of my life.

Kellie and I made our way to the school bus because the weather was getting bad. One by one our team members got on the bus and everyone was excitedly sharing stories and celebrating. After several more minutes, we all noticed three people missing, Fred, Liz, and Randi. We had all been worried about Randi because of the setback she experienced with the bronchitis so we waited. Finally, Randi got on the bus crying. Was she happy? Was she sad? Did she finish or drop out? "I finished the race," she shouted and everyone cheered for her. She sat down next to me and continued to try to hold back her emotions as she said, "Danny, I have to tell you what happened. They were amazing, Fred and Liz were amazing. I made it to mile eleven and my calves started to cramp so I sat down. I had not seen any Southside team members for a long time and felt alone. I knew I was going to have to drop out because of my legs. Out of nowhere, Fred and Liz show up and start saying things like, 'Get up, let's go, we will stay with you, but you will finish this race.' I told them to please just LEAVE ME ALONE. I told them to go on and finish the race without me. They pointed to a stop sign about a quarter of a mile down the road and told me to get up and just go to the stop sign and then sit back down if I wanted to. So I did. I made it to the stop sign and went way past it and then sat down again because of my legs. Once again I asked them to go *"I told them to please just leave me alone."* on and please LEAVE ME ALONE. They kept saying, 'Twenty-one started and twenty-one will finish.' Liz pointed out a street sign not too far away and told me to get up and walk to the street sign and then take another rest saying, 'We will stay with you.' So I got up again and made it to the street sign and was able to keep going. By now I was past the twelve mile marker and it had started to storm but it didn't matter because I was physically unable to take another step. A metro police officer working the race rode up on his horse and pointed right at me. He told me to get off the road because I was moving too slowly and the slow runners were being cleared from the race due to the weather. Fred jumped between me and the officer and said, 'We've got her. We will take care of her,' and the officer rode off. Liz immediately started encouraging me to get up. She pointed out how close we were to the finish line and that most of the way was downhill. Once again, she somehow talked me into standing up and giving it another try. I grabbed both of their hands the last few steps and hugged both of them as we crossed the finish line. I could not believe I made it! Without Fred and Liz staying after me, I would never have finished."

I was so proud of Randi and our team. Her story serves as a perfect example of what many of our students need from us. Did Fred and Liz pick Randi up in a wheelbarrow and push her the last two miles? No, that would be enabling and Randi would not have been filled with a sense of accomplishment. She did all the work herself, took every step on her own.

In your school, do you make your students earn their way or are you massaging their grades and moving them on because they are too old? Did Fred and Liz give up on Randi because she was discouraged and struggling? Did they leave her alone because she was taking up too much of their time and energy? No, they tenaciously stayed after her and did not allow dropping out as an option. In your school, do you allow students the option of dropping out? Don't ever say, "You are old enough now to decide for yourself and if you choose to just sit there and do nothing, then you have chosen to fail." Or, does every teacher and adult staff member view themselves as SWEEPERS of student success? A clean sweep means you have to go back and get what is behind and continue to sweep, sweep, sweep…and just keep sweeping.

Chapter Twenty-Three

AGGRESSIVE CARE

Kellie was fourteen, Amy twelve, and Zach was eight years old when we received the news that their mom and my wife Debbie had an aggressive form of breast cancer. I could not function at work. The Big Bad Wolf was breathing down my neck and I was running scared. I can still hear the voice of the Wolf using his if/ then threats, "If Debbie dies, then you will not be able to raise these kids by yourself, especially the two girls. You do not know how to do make-up. You know nothing about girls' hair. These kids need their mom. You cannot raise them by yourself!" Fear had me in its grasp and I felt helpless.

"We are going to hit this cancer with everything we've got. Her cancer is the aggressive type so we will fight it AGGRESSIVELY!" Dr. Diana Shipley, our oncologist, said and filled us with hope. She had a specific and effective plan of action based on the most recent research. Her confident attitude shut the Big Bad Wolf up and sent him packing. It was not okay for Dr. Shipley to have any error in her thinking! Her aggressive approach meant that she was "combat ready" and willing to engage. I am so thankful they hammered my wife's cancer aggressively based on truth from the most recent research. She is now cancer free!

Dr. Shipley's aggressive treatment included:
1. Surgery - Cutting the cancer out
2. Radiation - Cooking the cancer cells

3. Chemotherapy - Killing the cancer cells (and her hair)

4. Arimidex - Starving the cancer cells

5. Herceptin - Coating the cancer cells with a really cool drug that keeps the cells from reproducing

Just like cancer, student apathy can only be defeated with aggressive care. The experts at your school must be "combat ready." The former sense of helplessness must be replaced with a willingness to engage the enemy. In a Brick House, the adults hammer apathy with everything they've got and the necessary *infrastructure* includes:

1. *Declare War on Apathy* requires unity among all staff members.

2. *Accountability* and *responsibility* are tied to the ICU list.

3. The foundation is, *Every Student Completes Every Assignment.*

4. Tenaciously stay after all students and *Never Leave Them Alone.*

5. Use *Academic CPR* to revive student's academic heartbeat.

6. There must be *harmony in grading practice* and grades must *reflect learning.*

7. Your main purpose, student learning, is on the *top of everyone's mind.*

8. *Make every minute of every day count.*

9. The *crucial metamorphosis* of all assignments must be *practice for learning.*

10. *Harmony in the halls* is a priority so students are filled with *hope.*

11. Engage your toughest students using a *secondary survey.*

12. *Esprit de Corps* builds a verbal wall around your school.

13. Every adult in your Brick House views themselves as a *sweeper.*

My Brick House

Marv and Darlene met in high school, were loyal to each other through his days in Germany/France during WWII, married when he returned, and provided a loving home for their three boys, Terry, Danny, and Dave. We had a brick home, played ball, swam on the swim team in the summer,

attended church every Sunday, and discussed our day every night around the dinner table with a hot meal prepared by our wonderful mom, Darlene. Most Sundays we returned home from church to a home filled with the smell of a roast (usually beef because that was my dad's favorite) which Mom had put in the oven before we left. We always ate together. We always talked about everything. Mom and Dad got in our world and it seemed like that was all that really mattered to them. They never took off without us unless it was a business trip for a couple of days. Dad never went out at night because he was either playing catch with his three boys, throwing us passes (underhand when he got really tired), cutting the grass, or fixing something for Mom. We had very little money but did not realize that until we got older because we were soaked in unconditional love, acceptance, and hope from our parents. One Saturday night a month our family would load up chips and Kool-Aid in the car and drive 30 minutes to Nashville to get Krystal hamburgers. The burgers were tiny and square on steamed buns and placed in individual boxes for only 10 cents apiece! We stayed in the car as my dad went in to get the burgers. Dave, the youngest, wanted "ketchup only", Danny (middle child-me) "mustard only", Terry wanted "just pickle", mom "pickle and mustard – be sure they scrape those onions off", while Marv took his with "everything". Getting everybody's order right was important to dad and he was always patient with us. What love Darlene showed her three boys packing up chips, Kool-Aid, and napkins just so we could afford to "go out" for dinner!

When we had a test at school it was our routine to go with one of my parents, usually Mom, into the living room, shut the door so we could concentrate and go over the material as many times as necessary until we were ready for the test. "Everybody has parents like mine," I thought.

I was never hungry, never heard my parents argue, always had clean clothes, always got a haircut (until my senior year – hippie time), went to the dentist twice a year, went to church every Sunday, had two perfect grandmothers and one character of a grandfather, lots of aunts who loved me, lots of uncles who told funny stories, a clean house, and most of all love and acceptance every day of my life from Marv and Darlene.

I am eternally grateful for my Brick House. My passion is for every educator to block out the external distractions and enthusiastically build their classroom and school culture to be **Brick House** strong!

Also by Danny Hill

Power of ICU

This book takes the reader through the creation of ICU…Intensive Care Unit, from its inception in the classrooms and hallways of schools that resulted in "Every Student Completing Every Assignment." You will hear a practical approach, created by teachers, of how to have all students complete their assignments and create a healthy school culture focused on  student learning and accountability. Administrators say ***Power of ICU*** is excellent for staff book studies because it challenges traditional paradigms and poor educational practices.

ICU Database

MANAGING MISSING ASSIGNMENTS MADE EASY

Secure 24/7 Access

The ICU Database is web-based, so teachers can create, monitor, and manage missing assignments online anytime from any computer with internet access. Each teacher has their own username and password for easy, secure access.

The "Power of ICU" Culture

The ICU Database makes entering and managing missing assignments easy. You can even create an attachment (e.g. the assignment in electronic form – doc, pdf, etc.) for each missing assignment so stakeholders can easily print extra copies. Students can be grouped together and viewed in "filters" (e.g. grade level, academic discipline, athletics, band, choir, clubs, at-risk, etc.) so everyone can become involved in reviving student engagement and responsibility.

Stakeholder Notifications

When a teacher puts a student's missing assignment on the ICU list, the student's parents are automatically emailed and texted a notification of the missing assignment. And, the email includes any specified comments or attachments from the teacher.

Easy Setup

You send us a list of teachers and students, we do the rest! Once a school signs up, we'll send a list of suggested data fields to include with your lists. Most schools assign a technical point-person at the school or district level who has the ability to export data from their student information system or a school-based technology specialist.

Customer Service & Support

We're here to help! Support is available by phone or email. Because the ICU Database is web-based we can provide remote support and make adjustments for you on the fly.

For more information, screenshots, or a demo of
the ICU Database visit www.poweroficu.com.

About the Author: Danny Hill

Danny Hill is a nationally respected authority on student apathy and school culture. He has taught science, economics, history, health, and coached football and basketball. He served four years as a high school assistant principal in charge of student management and curriculum. Danny was appointed principal of Southside, a large K-8 school, where he remained for twenty years. Under his leadership, Southside grew into a highly respected school that enjoyed a positive reputation with the faculty, students, parents and community.

Danny has presented to over 100,000 educators in twenty states and is also a motivational speaker, teacher, author, and educational consultant. He co-founded and is Chief Manager of JJ&ZAK LLC. He and his wife and family live in Middle Tennessee.